The Thing
You Think
You Cannot Do

Also by Gordon Livingston

Only Spring: On Mourning the Death of My Son

Too Soon Old, Too Late Smart:
Thirty True Things You Need to Know Now

And Never Stop Dancing:
Thirty More True Things You Need to Know Now

How to Love: Choosing Well at Every Stage of Life

The Thing You Think You Cannot Do

Thirty Truths about Fear and Courage

Gordon Livingston, M.D.

Da Capo
∞
LIFE
LONG

A Member of the Perseus Books Group

Published by Da Capo Press
A member of the Perseus Books Group
www.dacapopress.com

Library of Congress Cataloging-in-Publication Data is available for this book.

ISBN 978-0-7382-1552-5 (hardcover)
ISBN 978-0-7382-1579-2 (eBook)
ISBN 978-0-7382-1650-8 (paperback)

Da Capo Press books are available at special discounts for bulk purchases in the U.S. by corporations, institutions, and other organizations. For more information, please contact the Special Markets Department at the Perseus Books Group, 2300 Chestnut Street, Suite 200, Philadelphia, PA 19103, or call (800) 810-4145, ext. 5000, or e-mail special.markets@perseusbooks.com.

Editorial production by Marathon Production Services. www.marathon.net

Set in 12-point Dante

First Da Capo Press edition 2012
First Da Capo Press paperback edition 2013

10 9 8 7 6 5 4 3 2 1

To Clare, the bravest person I have ever known.

And to Lucas, our son.

Contents

Introduction • xi

1. *It is dying that makes life important.* • 1

2. *Fear is the death of reason.* • 15

3. *Matters of the heart (or of state) that begin with a lie rarely end well.* • 21

4. *You have never suffered enough.* • 30

5. *Sometimes courage is hoping against hope.* • 38

6. *Old age is the revenge of the ugly.* • 48

7. *In life beyond high school, no one gives you credit for effort.* • 54

8. *Fear lurks behind perfectionism.* • 61

9. *Courage is not a feeling; it is a habit.* • 68

Contents

10. *Beware of ideas on which we all agree.* • 74

11. *There is no humor in heaven.* • 81

12. *Determination in the pursuit of folly is the indulgence of fools.* • 87

13. *Courage can be taught only by example.* • 95

14. *Nothing prepares us for the terrible risk of intimacy.* • 101

15. *Life is not a rehearsal.* • 108

16. *Courage is like love; it must have hope to nourish it.* • 115

17. *Punishment and revenge are the favored responses of fearful people.* • 121

18. *Life shrinks or expands in proportion to one's courage.* • 125

19. *Cowardice is the incapacity to love anything but oneself.* • 131

20. *Honesty is a prerequisite for courage.* • 136

Contents

21. *Fear springs from ignorance.* • 142

22. *It is pointless to fear the past.* • 149

23. *There are wounds that doctors cannot reach, that gratitude cannot heal.* • 155

24. *Courage is required to bear the unbearable.* • 159

25. *Ignorance can be remedied; stupidity has no cure.* • 163

26. *Heroism is sometimes stubbornness in the face of adversity.* • 167

27. *Life is not a spectator sport.* • 173

28. *One of the greatest risks is to be honest with ourselves.* • 178

29. *At the heart of anger is sadness.* • 183

30. *The quest for courage is a journey within.* • 190

Acknowledgments • 199

Introduction

Fear is the central issue of our time. Once an adaptive emotion that protected our ancestors on the plains of Africa, fear has become a corrosive influence in modern life, eroding our ability to think clearly. Exploited for power by our political leadership and for money by the media, fear is embedded in the way we think about our lives.

Our preoccupation with "safety" is a natural reaction to our vulnerability to loss. At the same time, the search for perfect safety is absurd given the inevitability of our eventual demise.

Even as our lives have become safer overall, our fears remain intact and lie at the foundation of our most revered institutions, notably religion, which typically promises some version of immortality as a salve for our dread of extinction.

Americans live in an increasingly authoritarian society out of persistent fear that other tribes in distant places are a threat to our way of life, to our very existence. Over the last century, this apprehension has brought us to a continual state of war, which shows no sign of abating. And, although we congratulate ourselves for being a peace-loving people, our national anthem is a tribute to fighting off threatening foreigners. (Because I am, by accident of birth, an American, the reader will find that most societal references in this book derive from this place and time. However, I have tried to choose themes with universal meaning and application.)

As a psychiatrist, I spend my professional life in the presence of fearful people. An entire category of mental disorders is characterized by "anxiety," a distress of the mind typified by worry and dread. This disorder is usually distinguished from fear by the fact that anxiety may have no specific object, except when it takes the form of so-called phobias: of crowds, of flying, or of driving, for example. When anxiety is acute, its physiological symptoms are identical to those of fear: sweating, rapid heartbeat, muscular tension. We are, in short, manifesting the once-adaptive "fight-or-flight" phenomenon except that neither of these responses may now be called for. More common triggers in the present day are things such as public speaking, taking a test, or rejection in love. Fears of failure and humiliation have replaced the threat of imminent death as our most common sources of apprehension.

Collectively, our fears take the form of a pervasive worry that supports huge therapeutic and pharmaceutical industries devoted to the alleviation of emotional distress. Because I work in one of these industries, I routinely employ medications, but I have found myself in recent years invoking virtues such as courage and resilience as alternatives to the sense of victimization and helplessness that medical diagnoses often engender. On the wall of my office hangs a 1915 picture of the British explorer Ernest Shackleton's ship *Endurance* trapped in the ice of the Weddell Sea, near Antarctica. His ultimately successful battle for his crew's survival has much to teach us about the courage required to confront adversity of all sorts.

What are we afraid of and what can we do about it? A partial list of fears that I deal with in those seeking psychotherapy include: fear of dying, fear of change, fear of intimacy, fear of loss, fear of failure, fear of success, fear of inadequacy, fear of time, fear of loneliness, fear of the unknown. With a little thought you can doubtless make your own list. Interestingly, anxiety, like its frequent companion, depression, appears to have an element of heritability. You are more likely to suffer excessive apprehension if other members of your biological family are similarly afflicted. No one is sure how this predisposition passes from one generation to the next or on what chromosome(s) it is manifest. Although we will probably find the answer over the next few years, will we then have learned anything about alleviating anxiety itself?

This biological inclination is the reason that most treatment for anxiety includes the use of one medication or another. Drugs that increase serotonin levels in the brain, the SSRI antidepressants, are effective against chronic anxiety. Minor tranquilizers such as Xanax, Ativan, and Klonopin provide significant short-term relief but have the disadvantage of chemical dependency. Psychotherapy also frequently helps, and it is about this process and what it teaches that I will have more to say. The best psychological antidote to anxiety turns out to be some combination of hope and courage. How these virtues are acquired, manifested, and taught are at the core of this book. It is not easy to live a courageous life, and no one is brave all the time or in every circumstance.

Accepting our own mortality becomes most problematic in our middle years. We seek to slow the aging process and to embody the misleading adage that "you are only as old as you feel." Some people panic and imagine that they can recapture their youth with new activities, possessions, or relationships. In the movie *Moonstruck,* someone asks at the dinner table, "Why do men cheat?" The Olympia Dukakis character replies simply, "fear of death."

In middle age we confront our limitations and the slow demise of our dreams. Our best hopes for ourselves have been tested against reality and customarily found wanting. The love of our youth no longer resembles the image in the wedding pictures, nor do we. If we are lucky, we are bored; if unlucky, we impulsively rearrange (and often ruin) our lives. If we are like many people, we have already divested ourselves of our first spouse and are dissatisfied with our second (or third). Too cynical, you say? Look at the divorce statistics and count the couples you know who are truly happy. Our children need us less and our jobs do not usually promise excitement, yet we are glad to have them. We may even be less successful than our parents. We wonder what happened to the universal hope for generational upward mobility.

A surprising number of Americans are depressed. In the adult population, 9.5 percent, or 22 million people, will suffer from clinical depression in any given year. The dividing line between existential sadness or discouragement and the kind of depression for which medication is recommended are blurred. As evidence, 54 million of us are on antidepressants at any given moment. Some of this number may be the result of overprescribing, but most epidemiologists believe that clinical depression is diagnosed and treated less often than it occurs.

In the face of this malaise, an argument can be made that we live in a culture of fear. For example, we are consumers of advertising that is focused on the proposition that material possessions, including pharmaceutical products, can compensate for feelings of inadequacy, creating the illusion that we can buy (or at least rent) happiness.

Many American cultural icons are wealthy people who display a relentless selfishness, and the growing disparity between the rich and the middle class (not to mention the 12.6 percent of the country living in poverty) is a testimony to our failure to look after one another in any responsible way. Here's another statistic to ponder: The poorest 20 percent of Americans earn 3.4 percent of the national income; the richest 20 percent earn 49.4 percent. That ratio, 14.5 to 1, is the highest it has ever been. The street protests of the aggrieved "99 percent" testify to a growing public consciousness of the unfairness in income distribution and political influence, not just in the United States but also worldwide.

Our proudest value, the rationale for all our wars, is freedom. But what about other values such as courage, hope, charity, and justice? An unsparing look at what we have become—a devout, militarized, defensive, xenophobic, and selfish society—reveals a bleak picture. We need to see ourselves as we are if we are going to change this version of ourselves. Otherwise, we will continue to be manipulated by our fears, that is, by the angels of our baser nature.

I have spent some time at war and watched young men struggle with issues of prolonged fear, attachment, and meaning more vividly than is normally the case in our daily lives. Discovering who reacted with steadfastness and concern for others under the threat of imminent death was often surprising. Nearly everyone is afraid in combat. (Those few who are not are in a special category and are dangerous to themselves and those around them. In *Moby Dick,* Starbuck says, "I will have no man in my boat who is not afraid of a whale.") Overcoming the fear of death to act on behalf of the unit is the military definition of valor.

Courage can take many other forms, few of which result in medals. Moral courage, for example, was called by

Robert Kennedy "a more rare commodity than bravery in battle or great intelligence." Someone who sacrifices his reputation or career on behalf of an ideal is seldom celebrated. A government employee who resigns rather than carries out an unlawful order. A whistleblower who exposes corporate malfeasance. A soldier who makes public the secrets of an illegitimate war. All take risks on behalf of their fellow citizens and the truth.

This book is about personal traits and values and how they are taught and exhibited. Any discussion of fear and courage has political overtones because the philosophies we admire and adopt individually find inevitable expression in our choice of leaders. In a democracy, our ideals are both shaped and reflected by those we elect to office. These larger issues are inseparable from the ways in which we experience our lives at a personal level. One does not have to be a political scientist to see this connection.

Throughout the book, I explore the crucial questions of how we deal with fear at both an individual and a societal level. We routinely face situations that make us anxious, that test our convictions about ourselves and what we wish our lives to be. In our everyday decisions, we either accept the limitations that fear would impose upon us or refuse to be cowed and so act in ways congruent with our deepest values and fondest hopes.

We are not what we say, or how we feel, or what we think. *We are what we do.* Fear is both a noun and a verb, an emotion and a way of engaging (or not engaging) those around us. Courage is manifest by action; it is habitual and the only nonpharmacologic antidote to the apprehension that is inevitable in an uncertain and often dangerous world.

And finally, I have learned this: A working sense of humor may be our last, best defense against fear. Remember those who declared after 9/11 that "everything has changed" and we would not laugh again?

How wrong they were.

You gain strength, courage, and confidence by every experience in which you really stop to look fear in the face. You must do the thing which you think you cannot do.

—Eleanor Roosevelt

It is dying that makes life important.

I'm not afraid of death;
I just don't want to be there when it happens.
—Woody Allen

Death is the fundamental fear from which most of the others derive. Every sentient creature struggles against the threat of extinction. What makes humans unique (so far as we know) is the ability to contemplate our demise. From this comes our longing for immortality and our fondness for religion that promises everlasting life. We struggle against the relentless passage of time with its attendant losses, all of which are rehearsals for the final loss of ourselves. However unsuccessfully we have dealt with fear in our lives (usually by avoidance or distraction), most of us have a final chance to be brave in the way we face our deaths.

Used to explain everything from cowardice in battle to our persistent search for perfect love, the consciousness of death is never far from the surface. Although most of us hold it at bay when we are young through the use of what might be called healthy denial, the shadow of our mortality is what lends intensity to the present moment. We construct elaborate belief systems to soften the finality of death and ascribe to each person a soul that outlives us. This longing for immortality is simultaneously the most comforting and the most divisive way that we assert our humanity. Worshipping a god who gives us rules to follow to attain everlasting life is not enough. Instead, we declare that the gods worshipped by those unlike ourselves are illegitimate, and out of this intolerance has come appalling violence.

Few believers can see themselves as accidental victims of childhood indoctrination, born to particular parents in a particular place and time, raised to believe in their parents' god to the exclusion of all others, part of a tribal group of fellow believers who feel threatened by the knowledge that their beliefs are not universal, that in other places people pray to different gods with the same hope and fervor and exclusivity that we feel. These others are not just wrong and condemned to eternal perdition but also frequently seen as dangerous and eager to impose their beliefs on us, through violence if necessary. More than territory or resources or power, differences in religion account for a staggering share of the destruction that human beings have visited on one another. Some claim that the great wars of the twentieth century were not religious. But political systems, language, and ethnicity all represent equivalent beliefs, secular religions, that distinguish one group of people from another and undermine our sense of common humanity. We can classify groups as "the other" and less deserving of life in many ways; religion is still prominent among them in our twenty-first-century world.

Little public attention is focused on the question of the importance of *meaning* in our lives. When asked to describe what their lives mean beyond a desire to get ahead, most Americans fall back on some religious formulation. We are a churchy country, more so than almost any developed society. When polled, 96 percent of us say that we believe in God and so believe in some form of life after death in which the good are rewarded and the wicked punished. This belief in a better afterlife allows us to tolerate a lot of earthly unhappiness and inequity and mitigates against behavior toward other people that would instill a sense of meaning in our lives right now.

Whatever heaven we believe awaits us, few seem in a hurry to get there. A large element of subconscious doubt about immortality is expressed by the way we cling to whatever life we know, no matter how burdensome or unhappy it may be. In this we are like other animals that presumably have no concept of a soul or life everlasting. No matter our belief systems, we share with them a primitive fear of nonexistence. The difference is that we must live our entire lives with the anticipation of death. What is required of us to accept our mortality and retain hope in a future in which we will not participate?

❧

People suffering from anxiety—fear without a specific object—routinely become subject to panic attacks characterized by frightening physical sensations: rapid heartbeat, hyperventilation, sweating, and a sense that they are about to die. Hospital emergency departments regularly encounter patients with these symptoms. Sometimes these episodes have a trigger, an auto accident, for example. Often no precipitant is discernible; people wake up from a sound sleep gasping for air. Although it may seem reassuring to tell such people that tests confirm that nothing is wrong with their hearts, customarily they remain terrified of a recurrence of these feelings.

No one lives an anxiety-free life. Like other forms of pain, anxiety is a warning that something is amiss, so anxiety is useful if it helps identify the imbalance and stimulates an effort to correct it. Such corrections usually require some combination of medication and psychotherapy. Left untreated, recurrent anxiety can shrink a life, sometimes to the confines of one's own house. Short of this outcome, a person's freedom to operate in the world can become so severely limited that he or she avoids situations that are likely to provoke even mild anxiety: crowds, driving, crossing bridges, and the like. Such avoidance behaviors increase fears and promote withdrawal.

Truly life-threatening situations can produce reactions identical to a panic attack. However, the military has discovered that through training and unit cohesion one can overcome fear and learn to function even when bullets are cracking nearby. One can, in other words, train people to be brave by convincing them that their survival depends on their courage. At its best, psychotherapy is another form of training people to confront their deepest fears while clarifying the unhappy consequences of avoidance.

Tolerance for risk is an individual characteristic. Some people seek out danger and enjoy the "adrenaline rush" provided by leaping from airplanes, climbing walls of rock, or otherwise embracing activities that terrify most of us. As a whole, our society is risk averse. "Safety first" has become a mantra, plastered on trucks and on workplace walls. We are grateful to the police for taking risks on our behalf, but even they are a part of a culture that favors caution and safety over courage and daring. SWAT teams took four hours to enter and clear Columbine High School after the shooters were dead, and at least one wounded person inside bled to death while waiting for help. The police in Norway exercised similar caution in approaching an island where a man with an assault rifle was methodically shooting young people. When Cheshire, CT, police in 2007 arrived at a home where they knew a family was being held by two men, they elected to wait for backup even as a mother and two daughters were being murdered and the house set on fire. Routine police procedures have as a major goal the safety of the police, sometimes at the expense of the citizens they are there to protect.

We are preoccupied with safety in our daily lives and imagine that some set of cautious behaviors will protect us from harm. Presumed threats to our security become magnified—crime, drugs, terrorism—while the real dangers to our survival—accidents, lifestyle choices, heart disease, and cancer—do not inhabit our nightmares until we or someone we love is affected by them. Our failure to address the issue of climate change represents the most vivid example of dangerous denial.

Life is intrinsically unsafe. We can buckle our seatbelts and wear our bicycle helmets. We can stop smoking and take to the road in our running shoes. We can walk our children to the school bus and secure them in their car seats. But death will get us anyway, sooner or later. (One commentator suggested that with all the emphasis on diet and exercise, in the future people will be lying around hospitals dying of nothing.) None of us can avoid this knowledge; it informs our lives even as we try not to think about it and struggle to deny it by changing our appearances and worshiping at the altar of youth. Our fear of death also causes us to react with shock and anger when people die suddenly or in large numbers. When a plane crash occurs, we investigate and search for ways to make sure it will never happen again. When, inevitably, it does, the National Transportation Safety Board conducts another painstaking investigation. The result is an air travel system that has a steadily improving safety record, which is certainly reassuring if you are about to walk into a metal tube that will transport you to five miles above the earth and hurtle you toward your destination at six hundred miles per hour. Yet the fantasy of perfect safety continues to elude us, and every now and then one of those metal tubes falls out of the sky.

Much riskier is an activity we consider more prosaic: driving our cars. Each year about forty thousand Americans are killed while driving, but we fear it less than flying because we remain earthbound. Less investigation is required because automobile accidents and the deaths they cause are considered by most of us as routine events—as long as they are happening to others. Although we consider building safer cars important and our seatbelt use is now at 85 percent, we also tune out most safe driving campaigns and the ubiquitous "Baby on Board" signs remain a public celebration of fertility.

A big problem in dealing with our fears is our poor record when evaluating which ones are grounded in reality and which are misplaced or exaggerated. We are notoriously poor at risk assessment. We buy guns for protection, for example, while statistics demonstrate that a gun in the house is much more likely to kill someone who lives there than the intruder of our nightmares.

We have been through seasons in which certain well-publicized threats—shark attacks, killer bees, satanic cults in nursery schools—have come and gone. Other persistent apprehensions are more enduring but of little validity: road rage, Internet stalking, vaccines, school shootings, being killed by terrorists. Not only does this cause us unnecessary anxiety, it renders us subject to manipulation by those who benefit, monetarily or politically, from our fears. *Frightened people do not make good decisions.* In the first decade of the twenty-first century, America became embroiled in two lengthy wars that were essentially fearful responses to the attacks of 9/11. Our media magnify threats, crime for example, to keep us watching the news. Most people have a highly exaggerated fear of being the victim of violence because the airways are saturated with such reports. In the parlance of TV news, "If it bleeds, it leads." In fact, violent crime has been decreasing in most places over the last ten years. Truth, it turns out, is frequently a matter of emphasis.

We lose track of the true meaning of courage, a virtue that requires *both choice and risk*. A pilot who makes a skillful landing on the Hudson River becomes a hero even though he had no choice if he was to save himself. A surgeon who saves a life is hailed as heroic even though he took no risk. Both the pilot and the surgeon protest that "I was just doing my job," and we consider them modest rather than truthful.

In idealizing everyone who wears a uniform, we demonstrate how much we need heroes even if we have to construct them out of whole cloth. The false stories about the heroism of Pvt. Jessica Lynch and Cpl. Pat Tillman, even the initial reports of the desperate "firefight" in the Bin Laden compound, are examples of the routine exaggerations of courage that are common in war.

Stories of real heroism, such as the actions on 9/11 of the passengers on Flight 93 who organized themselves to die fighting rather than passively ride to their deaths, the man who jumps onto a subway track to save a stranger, the bystander who throws himself into the freezing Potomac River to rescue survivors of a plane crash, are rightly recognized as exceptional.

Obviously, courage can take many forms. The sudden burst of physical risk that characterizes most bravery on the battlefield is different from the long-term dedication to principle that we think of as moral courage. Exhibiting one form of courage does not imply that one will be brave in other ways as well. We are all familiar with the stories of war heroes whose later lives collapsed in dishonesty or the cases of highly decorated soldiers who return from combat and murder their wives.

Perhaps the highest form of valor is the dedication to principle that requires both contemplation and determination over time. Sacrifices on behalf of others are often seen in those who choose religious vocations. The capacity for commitment that is implied in such choices may be motivated by some expectation of divine reward, but turning one's back on the pleasures of the world to improve the lives of others is the very definition of altruism. So perhaps the concept of *benefit to others* ought to be added to the elements of risk and choice in defining courageous behavior. This definition would eliminate those who climb mountains alone or parachute off tall buildings, acts that require a kind of bravery (or foolhardiness) but are ultimately self-centered and are of no use, excepting entertainment, to anyone else.

It is within ourselves, where we confront our deepest fears and insecurities, that we find our own forms of courage or cowardice. Like any virtue, bravery is manifest in our habitual actions. Fidelity to an ideal, risking ourselves to stand up for the powerless, refusing to crumble beneath the weight of time, all require a steadfastness that is uncommon in a culture dominated by glamour, celebrity, and instant gratification. *Esse quam videri*, to be and not to seem, is a dated but admirable motto seldom manifested by the movie stars and sports personalities who inhabit our fantasies of success.

Doctors, in whom people are taught to place their trust, are routinely disciplined for taking financial or sexual advantage of their patients and for providing substandard care. Air traffic controllers, even pilots, have been discovered sleeping on the job. Soldiers have been convicted of war crimes, but a uniform at the airport elicits statements of appreciation and sometimes a first-class upgrade. Support for the troops can become support for the war that is killing them.

Bravery, like fear, is contagious. A big part of military training involves building unit cohesion, a mutual affection for and dependency on the people with whom you serve. Soldiers on the battlefield do not exhibit a lot of patriotic fervor, about which many of them are openly cynical; instead, they speak of the obligation they feel to the people around them. This loyalty is most frequently the basis for acts of heroism. Certain populations appear to have an indomitable spirit, notably the English during the World War II bombing raids by Germany, and the Israelis in the face of terrorism.

Contrast the steadfastness displayed by these populations and the American response to 9/11, which most resembled a national anxiety attack in which we imagined that our entire way of life was being threatened by a relatively small and stateless group of radical Islamists. By declaring that we were in a war for survival, we became more like them: angry, intolerant, ethnocentric, and willing to employ violence to promote our ideology. Vengeance drove us though we labeled it justice, and we effectively altered parts of our constitution relating to extralegal detentions, torture, and abrogation of our own civil rights as we tried to recapture our sense of safety and invulnerability.

And what price did we pay for all of the above? Over six thousand American dead, twice as many as perished in 9/11. At least two hundred thousand diagnosed with traumatic brain injury alone. More than one hundred thousand Afghanis and Iraqis dead. And three trillion dollars that might have been spent on health care, education, or retiring the national debt. All that money, of course, has been borrowed. I think of these irreplaceable lives and colossal sums as the wages of fear. What have we gained? Are we safer now from terrorist attack than we were ten years ago? Do the radical Islamists really threaten our way of life? What have we learned about ourselves?

Our efforts to conquer our fears, or even to discern which ones are realistic, are impeded by what we see on our television screens and what we hear from our politicians. Everyone wants to be on the safe side, especially when we imagine that the threat is to our very existence. We cannot cope with our fear of death except by seeing it as a realistic apprehension that can, if we let it, provide a sense of urgency and a determination to extract pleasure and meaning from the present moment. Such moments, strung together, constitute our lives.

Fear is the death of reason.

I've developed a new philosophy . . .
I only dread one day at a time.
—Charlie Brown

A way of life that encourages living in the moment has a lot to recommend it. The past is unchangeable, the future unpredictable. What little we control in our lives can be exercised only right now. We like to think we behave rationally and that our actions are governed by a sober evaluation of consequences, but this idea ignores ample evidence that most of what we do is either habitual or the product of underlying motivations, emotions, impulses, and biases that constitute Freud's "unconscious mind." No better example exists than our buying behavior, in which we are routinely manipulated by sophisticated forms of marketing that appeal to our unfulfilled longings to be someone other than who we are: richer, younger, thinner, and with more hair, fewer wrinkles, and more friends.

What is the downside of a billion-dollar industry devoted to creating this chronic dissatisfaction with ourselves? This relentless consumerism focuses on the most superficial aspects of what it means to be human: how we look and what we own. A preoccupation with these attributes is the definition of self-absorption. The results of adopting such values can be seen in the most fundamental institution of society, marriage. On what do we base our decisions about whom to marry? Whenever a survey is done on the subject, the results show an interesting gender difference. Men are drawn to women who fit a rather narrow definition of physical attractiveness; women look for a good provider.

Half of marriages end in divorce, but what of those that endure? How many of them have provided lasting satisfaction to both partners? Research in this area is difficult because long-married couples are reluctant to disclose that they have made a mistake that has lasted most of their lives. If we want to be generous, we could hope that at least half of those in unions that have persisted are reasonably satisfied with their choice. (Many reasons other than emotional fulfillment—children and finances to name two—impel people to remain together.) We are still confronted with the uncomfortable truth that marriage, the building block and economic engine of society, has a failure rate, as defined by mutual satisfaction, of at least 75 percent. Still, as the popularity of Internet dating sites attests, practically all of us want to be married.

If it is true that *ideas are easier to love than people*, perhaps it is the image of perfect love that draws us onward to our next relationship. For many of us who had good mothers, the memory of unconditional acceptance lives on in our subconscious as our deepest longing. Because this effortless experience of being valued just as we are is hard to replicate in our adult lives, we are taught that we must settle for something less. How much less is at the heart of most marital difficulties. The fact that we keep trying, however, attests to another of our deepest fears: loneliness.

In the hell that is prison, what further punishment can be used to motivate people who have already lost nearly everything that renders life worthwhile? The answer is solitary confinement. No better example exists of the importance of human connections, even in the most extreme circumstances. What allows one to get from day to day in a loud, dangerous, soul-numbing environment where one's freedom and choice of companions is so restricted, a place devoid of most of what we think of as attachment or caring? Even here, something is worse: solitude.

Little wonder then that our daily lives contain so many behaviors directed at establishing and maintaining a sense of connectedness with at least one other person. Other fears—death, humiliation, rejection—have in common the fact that we will do practically anything to avoid being alone. There is no emptier sound than the door closing behind us in a place we inhabit by ourselves.

I work with many patients who have as a part of their unhappiness the conviction that when they were young, shallow, and uninformed, they made a choice of life partner that they have come to regret. Sometimes this unhappy outcome represents a mistake in judgment for which they now must pay a price. Often that price takes the form of an agonizing choice between breaking up a family or continuing an unsatisfying marriage. But often what is happening reveals a *fear of intimacy*.

Here is how that story frequently goes: We are inclined in our closest relationships to replay our childhood conflicts. If one or both of our parents was unduly intrusive and controlling, we learn to have little confidence in our own judgments. We also tend to experience love as something that must be earned and traded like a commodity. This is the concept of contingent reinforcement: If we do certain things—get good grades, excel athletically, abide by parental rules—we feel secure and loved. If we misbehave or let our parents down, we anticipate a withdrawal of that love. This withholding is more painful than any punishment or limit setting that we may experience. The outcome of such a philosophy, particularly if it leads to adolescent power struggles, is a sense of love as a form of manipulation, a reward for good behavior.

If we take this learning into our adult relationships (and why wouldn't we?), we adopt a "contractual" sense of what it is to love and be loved: If you do this for me, I'll do that for you. This philosophy is inimical to the idea of true intimacy, in which the line between giving and receiving is blurred. And here is the fear: *If I become too dependent upon another person, they may take advantage of me. I retain my ability to get what I want only by a process of negotiation and compromise.* Mistrust, in other words, is built into the relationship.

This unfortunate assumption, that we get what we want only by demanding it, is one reason why people find themselves in the same unsatisfying relationships over and over again. Only people who have a similar self-protective view of love will engage us in this game. They too are afraid of real closeness, equating it with vulnerability and loss of control. And so the distance between people who have this fear grows larger as life becomes more complex and the demands of children and jobs require more and more negotiation. Our interactions become controlling, critical, and unkind. The distance between instinctive mistrust and alienation decreases with time until, like any form of paranoia, we become what we most fear and are truly alone.

Matters of the heart (or of state)
that begin with a lie rarely end well.

> *In the depth of winter, I finally learned that*
> *there was within me an invincible summer.*
>
> —Albert Camus

On September 11, 2001, I was at work when my wife called and told me to get to a television. It didn't take much watching to comprehend the likely magnitude of this tragedy; hundreds, perhaps thousands, would die. It was hard to know how to react, but I had a patient waiting to be seen and so went on with my day.

As it happened, I had a class scheduled early that afternoon at the Uniformed Services University of the Health Sciences, the military medical school. In 1969 I had what might charitably be described as a falling out with the Army when I was a doctor in Vietnam. So each year for the last twenty years I have spoken to medical students at USUHS about ethical conflicts inherent in military medicine. Around noon I got in my car and headed for the Naval Medical Center in suburban Washington, DC.

The first thing I noticed was that the traffic coming out of Washington was unexpectedly heavy for that time of day. Just to be sure that the class had not been cancelled, I called the medical school. No answer. Then I heard on the radio that the Pentagon had been attacked and concluded that all government business was finished for the day. What I didn't realize yet was that official Washington was in the process of executing a maneuver that can only be described as "run for your life." I turned around and drove home.

In subsequent days and weeks, as the country tried to come to terms with the loss of three thousand of its citizens, we were further traumatized by the anthrax attacks that killed five people and made thousands of others wary about picking up their mail. The Washington area was subjected to the "DC Snipers," who killed thirteen before they were apprehended. In the further aftermath of 9/11, the stock market collapsed and several airlines went out of business for lack of passengers. We were, in short, well and truly terrorized.

What was striking about our reaction to this attack was the gap between our patriotic protestations ("home of the brave") and our behavior, which was driven by fear and a thirst for vengeance. We were eager to strike back at our attackers and rallied around our political leadership who promised to do so. Every single politician had to respond affirmatively to the question "Are we at war?" and it was but a moment before the B-52s were bombing and the tanks were rolling, albeit down the roads of a country that had nothing to do with the attacks. Anyone who suggested that the stateless terrorists who had brought down those buildings constituted a criminal conspiracy that might better be dealt with through law enforcement or unconventional military forces was shouted down as insufficiently patriotic. This was Pearl Harbor, and these terrorists were the twenty-first-century equivalent of the Empire of Japan. Our freedoms were under attack and our national existence was at stake. What, finally, do we have to show for the war on terror? Were we lied to? Have we relinquished anything of value in terms of our place in the world and our own self-respect as a constitutional democracy, a nation of laws, a champion of human rights?

One of the interesting sidelights of our response to the September 11 attacks was the reflex characterization of the terrorists as cowards. One can call them many things: murderers of the innocent, suicidal lunatics, religious fanatics, the embodiment of evil. But viewed objectively, it is hard to sustain an allegation of cowardice against men who were willing to sacrifice their lives for what they believed, however misguided and homicidal they may have been. Part of our rage could be attributed to the fact that they could not be brought to justice because they had inflicted the death penalty on themselves. So we grabbed as many people as we could who looked like them and appeared to believe the same things, tortured many of them, and threw them in foreign prisons without due process. What does it mean to each of us to be a citizen of a country that, for a time at least, had as its national policy the torture of other human beings? Such are the wages of fear.

Contrast this with the elevation of our own soldiers to the status of heroes for the sacrifices they were prepared to make in the service of their country. Aware of the experience of veterans of Vietnam, who were not welcomed home with much enthusiasm after their service in

Matters of the heart (or of state) that begin with a lie rarely end well.

that unpopular war, we have made sure that the young men and women we send to Central Asia are the recipients of our admiration and gratitude for their service. We demonstrated our admiration for the heroism of all in uniform. This gesture was made easier by the fact that no sacrifices were required of most of us. We could follow the advice of our president to "go shopping" while indulging our guilt about so much being required of so few by lionizing those who volunteered to take the risks of combat.

Reinstituting the draft, which is the fairest way of sharing the risks attendant to any military undertaking, is politically unsustainable. The sons and daughters of the rich and powerful do not, in general, volunteer to serve. In 2007, by one count, 11 of the 635 members of Congress had children serving in the military, mirroring the inequities in service participation of the Vietnam generation. Exercising our sense of self-preservation by avoiding risk is one thing; asking others to hazard themselves for us in the belief that by annointing them "warriors" and applauding them in public we have somehow done our part to support them is another.

When I returned from Vietnam, I thought that nobody owed me anything for what I had seen and done. I no longer believed that the country was any more secure or our freedoms enhanced by my service. Nobody spit on me or called me a baby killer nor do I know of anyone who was subjected to such mythological indignities. In fact, most people didn't care what we had done and seen.

A lot of returnees had a nearly instinctive sense that all those lives lost and all the pain we had inflicted on ourselves and the little country we used to "contain communism" had been wasted. No important national interest had been served. For more than ten years, we had all been pawns in a colossal misjudgment on the part of our political leadership. I remember a cynical bumper sticker on a veteran's pickup truck back in the '70s: "Southeast Asian War Games, Second Place." Now at reunions of Vietnam veterans, it is fashionable to reminisce about our service there, remember the comradeship and the intensity that the dangers of combat gave to our lives, and declare that we were betrayed by the peace movement and politicians at home, not defeated on the battlefield.

The damaged men and women who have returned from similar ill-defined missions in Iraq and Afghanistan have been, as we were, changed by the experience. Their incidence of Post-Traumatic Stress Disorder hovers around 20 percent. The increasing suicide rate among them is a vexing problem that the military struggles to come to grips with. The repeated deployments and lack of a draft fly in the face of any definition of a collective national commitment. When we think of these soldiers at all, it is to hail them as heroes. The more important question is, what do they think of themselves? And what do they think of those of us who have not shared their awful experiences and cannot understand what they have been through? Has some important national objective been accomplished that justifies their sacrifices? Have our freedoms really been at stake?

Maintaining a sense of unity among people in a diverse society is challenging because many seek to divide us for political or personal gain. But nothing has the power to unite us like fear. The real threat to our way of life that World War II represented brought us together in a massive commitment to defeat those who were making credible efforts to violently impose their philosophies on the rest of the world. We were prepared to sacrifice anything to defeat them, and we did. The many conflicts in which we have been engaged since have been, in contrast, wars of choice. Each one has been justified as necessary to defend our values, especially freedom, but viewed through the prism of history, it is difficult to see how we are freer (or safer) now than we were sixty-five years ago. The long "cold war" struggle with communism was won economically rather than on the battlefield, but it suited some need within us to have the Soviet Union as an enemy for fifty years while we cowered under our school desks in the shadow of "mutually assured destruction" (MAD). It is hard to see the radical Islamists as constituting the same level of threat, yet they frighten us into walking around airports in our stocking feet and turning out to rallies to prevent the building of mosques.

When will we get a grip on our reactions to the parade of malefactors who have always inhabited the world and the space under our beds? We live in dangerous times, as we always have. We are all subject to the realities of threatening outcomes and an unhappy ending to each of our stories. Perfect safety is an illusion, and a fear that we might lose the people and principles that mean the most to us is a natural reaction to life's uncertainties.

Consider the things we do that enhance or detract from our moral sense of ourselves. Every action we take has consequences that illuminate how closely our professed beliefs comport with our behavior. So it is with the

Matters of the heart (or of state) that begin with a lie rarely end well.

societies we create. If we allow the enemy of the moment to frighten us into actions that violate our core values, we have lost some essential faith in ourselves as a good and generous people.

You have never suffered enough.

The truth will set you free,
but not until it is finished with you.

—David Foster Wallace

Those who have suffered a catastrophic loss, such as the death of a child or spouse, often take slender consolation in the idea that they have "paid their dues" to God or to the universe and that no more sacrifices of this magnitude will be required of them. I indulged this fantasy for a time after my twenty-two-year-old son Andrew killed himself in the grip of bipolar illness some years ago. Surely, I thought, no further misfortune could befall me that would approach this. Seven months after Andrew's death, my six year-old-son Lucas was diagnosed with a particularly virulent form of leukemia. Six months later he too was dead.

What can we learn from such apparently random devastation? That there is no defense against the vagaries of chance in this life? That we are being tested by having our worst fears realized? That we need more lessons in powerlessness and humility? I couldn't figure it out. Then it began to dawn on me that there *is* nothing to figure out, that as Robert Frost (who lost four of his six children) said in his old age, "In three words I can sum up everything I have learned about life—it goes on." Such a conviction is at once both defenseless and liberating.

Nobody tells us when we are young that there are no limits to pain. Instead, most of us are allowed to indulge the fantasy that if we do well in school, work hard, and respect authority, we will be spared the crushing grief that is the fate of other people, those we don't know. It is doubtless just as well that we are not burdened with the gift of foresight. In the yearbook marking my fiftieth college reunion, I closed my brief autobiography with the paraphrase of a favorite song, "I wish somehow I didn't know now what I didn't know then."

A subset of the category we label "courage" is *resilience*, the capacity to respond to adversity with a determination not to be defeated by it. Anyone who has attended a meeting of The Compassionate Friends, an organization of bereaved parents, learns that people vary widely in their reactions to grief. About one-third of those who have sustained such a loss appear defeated by it. Their best hopes have been burned to ashes and they will never recover. For another third, time will do its work and they will struggle back to some semblance of their former selves. How long this process takes is individual and unpredictable. A third group manifests the reality proposed by Ernest Hemingway: "The world breaks everyone, and afterward, some are strong at the broken places." These are the people who plant the gardens, establish the memorial funds, accompany others in their mourning. They are more than survivors; they have prevailed.

One of these people, Elizabeth Edwards, was my friend. After the loss of her son Wade at sixteen in a car crash, she went on to establish a computer lab for high school students in his name. She became a national expert on health care, had two more children (one at forty-eight and the other at fifty), wrote two books (one of them titled *Resilience*), and was a model of what one bereavement expert has described as "a triumphant survivor." And yet she had yet more grief to endure, her husband's infidelity and her own losing battle against breast cancer. All of this she confronted head on and with a notable lack of self-pity. Her heart was broken but she was not, and she stayed in the fight until the very last.

Who among us can calculate the sum or purpose of human suffering? We are required by our nature and the imperative of human survival to attach ourselves to others who become our hostages to fate. This opens us to loss and to grief. We live with an instinctive doubt about the larger meaning of our lives. We survive in the hearts of others who love us, but we also know that when they are gone, so are we. Although we strive to be special, none of us leaves behind much of a footprint to mark our passage upon the earth. We inhabit a small planet in a minor solar system. We appear to be equidistant from the unfathomable distances of the universe and the submicroscopic particles of which we are made. And yet the questions of why we are here, how best to live, and the meaning of the losses that we endure remain answerable only by the bargains with life that each of us choose to strike.

We search for justice and find mainly random events. We watch the wicked prosper and the good suffer. We console ourselves with the idea of ultimate fairness on some other plane where each of us will be punished and rewarded according to his or her behavior on earth, but we lack evidence for that and so have to live with the imperfect justice that we mete out to each other. What terrifies us is the randomness that characterizes the systems for reward and punishment that we have created. The rich appear to have a better chance for success in almost every area, including the legal system. The inscription on the courthouse may read, "Equal justice under law," but few of us believe that this laudable goal is regularly achieved. American prisons are warehouses for the poor and uneducated and minority members of the society. Two million of our citizens are incarcerated, the highest percentage of any nation on earth. What does this say about us?

Any institution is a distillation of the dominant values of the society; our legal arrangements are no exceptions. Just as with our educational and health care systems, our laws and their application favor the wealthy. When a tornado passes through town, who is most at risk: the people in the trailer park or those living in the big houses? When a recession hits, who suffers the most? Living with such inequities indefinitely is impossible. Sooner or later the disparity in suffering either sparks collective outrage or results in the numbing of our critical faculties and the betrayal of our deepest values.

Our high incarceration rate indicates who and what we are afraid of. Apart from people who commit acts that have always been considered crimes—murder, theft, robbery, and so on—we have filled our jails with those who pose little threat to the rest of us. In 2002, 54.7 percent of federal prisoners were imprisoned for drug crimes. Our attempts to control the flow and use of illegal substances has been a colossal failure that has served mainly to increase the price of illegal drugs, enrich some of the most contemptible people in society, provoke a culture of death and violence in our inner cities, and swell our prison population without materially reducing the consumption of drugs or confronting the issues of addiction that drive such behavior. It is as if we learned nothing from our fourteen-year experience with the prohibition of alcohol, which, although it destroys many lives, is now freely available, relatively inexpensive and no longer the source of widespread crime. We can manage the millions of people who become addicted to alcohol without throwing them in jail or otherwise declaring war on a common human craving. We all also benefit from the taxes people pay to drink.

What we choose to punish people for is a good indication of what we fear. Apart from the prohibitions contained in the Ten Commandments, the complexity of modern society has required the punishment of crimes apparently unanticipated by God when he handed the tablets to Moses, notably sex offenses, including rape. An interesting commentary on our fears is that we imprison people for the misuse of controlled substances that are consumed for the sole reason that they make people feel better, albeit temporarily. To live peaceably with each other, we have decided that society must control certain appetites. If, as in the case of drugs, this control proves impossible, our response is to redouble our efforts. Imagine if all the money we spend interdicting the commercial flow of illegal substances and punishing those who use and sell them were turned to other purposes, starting with substance abuse treatment. (This same line of thinking has gained little traction when applied to our foreign wars.)

And so we suffer twice: in the broken lives and withered hopes of the addicted in their relentless pursuit of evanescent pleasure and in the suffering we as a society exact on those who use and traffic in these substances. We spend billions and distract law enforcement from other, more important crimes even as it becomes apparent that this is a war without end and without the prospect of victory. As with most of our wars, there are those who profit: the armed bureaucracies, the builders of jails, the makers of surveillance equipment, and the successful perpetrators of the crimes that we have created. The deeply moralistic streak within the society that yearns to prohibit "motivated behaviors," notably those driven by drugs and sex, becomes enshrined in our legal codes even as 17 percent of us die from obesity-related disorders and 20 percent of us still smoke. Drug prohibitions reflect irrational behavior that is not only ineffective but also manifests the fear that somewhere, somehow, someone is having a better time than we are. We all dread the forbidden appetites within ourselves that periodically burst into view. However, we no longer punish marital infidelity, which has come to be seen as a destructive behavior that ruins lives but is, in most cases, forgivably human. (If we prosecuted people for hypocrisy, think of the prisons we would need.) Would that we could be as tolerant and helpful with our other failed attempts to suppress our deepest desires. There is enough suffering to go around without criminalizing our frequent confusion about the difference between pleasure and happiness. The legal system is a blunt instrument with which to make this distinction.

5

Sometimes courage is hoping against hope.

*Whatever you are looking for
can only be found inside of you.*

—Rumi

Allison Caldwell was a young woman who, from the age of eleven, struggled with a rare, progressive, and ultimately fatal autoimmune disease called Wegener's granulomatosis. Although she was unable to attend school past sixth grade, her voracious reading and home-schooling by her mother turned Allison into an extremely well-educated young woman. She had a talent for architectural design that amazed professionals who examined her drawings and resulted in an elaborate LEGO construction that filled her basement with an entire town designed to her specifications and transformed into reality by her patient mother. Allison was also a world-class knitter who annually won first-place awards at the country's largest sheep and wool festival.

Allison had the good fortune to come under the care of Dr. Peter Rowe, Professor of Pediatrics at Johns Hopkins. His interest in and support of Allison over the fourteen years of her illness is an extraordinary example of compassion and dedication. Finally, Allison's mother, Jean, acquired skills equivalent to those of an intensive care nurse, enabling Allison to remain at home. Her body was confined to her bed by the pain and indignities of her illness, but her imagination and creativity ranged free.

Allison's lasting gift in her twenty-five years of life was to keep a detailed journal of her prolonged struggle to live as well as she could for as long as she could, the task that confronts us all. Following are excerpts from this journal over her last two years.

1/21/04   I was reading this book about Quakers. I am curious. It is a very low key, individual religion. A lot of it has to do with finding the strength to love within yourself.

Everything is very simple. I have read other books about religion. People always talk about how they find guidance in the bible. I guess I don't understand that. How is that supposed to help me deal with this illness? They talk a lot about love and how God is love. If God is love why would he, if it is a he, allow sickness to exist? It is hard to reconcile science to religion. Science can at least offer some proofs, evidence; religion requires only belief. I have always been one to ask questions. I have never felt lost. I just think that I have my own spiritual side. I don't see how praying will help me when I am freaking out; it just isn't practical; maybe it helps some people but I need a real person to talk to, someone to hear my thoughts, my frustrations, someone who can talk back to me. I can call Mom and she helps me. So my religion isn't any group or church, rather it is a congregation of me, my soul, all my inner strength, my own determination, my belief that I can deal with whatever comes along. I have a group of people who help me, who I can reach out to when life is too hard. Even in my darkest moments, I have to believe that my inner resolve will always be there and that my soul is uniquely mine and the belief in its strength will never let me down. I was born with this soul and I have relied on my determination to get me through and that is what I need to embrace. Those things come from within.

Sometimes courage is hoping against hope.

3/20/04   As time goes on everything seems to become more and more serious. It got serious with the kidney disease and then a few months later the Wegener's, and now the lungs and I wonder why. It is a useless wonder.

4/19/04   We are still reeling from what Dr. Rowe said about this illness being progressive and incurable. I think about it a lot. I think about all that I will leave behind. I think about all that I want to do. I think about what I want to do now. I think about what I want people to know. Then I panic, thinking that if I contemplate those things, it will make death real for me. I want Mom and Dad to know what a wonderful life they have given me. In some ways I am at peace with my death; in other ways I am driven to tears. I need to realize that the strength is in my spirit and soul, to know that my spirit is healthy and strong even as my body fails. Realizing all this has brought me to a place where I can have moments of peace.

9/29/04   My chemo is starting to beep and then we'll change all the IV stuff. Every day we go through this, no days off. The hardest part is that my life will not get any easier. There are times when I am just so afraid that I can't even explain it. I was looking at my cousin's wedding pictures. I always thought that someday I'd have my own wedding. I realize now all the

41

things that I'll never be able to do. I'm afraid now that things will get worse really fast.

11/11/04 I have been thinking about my life and how I really have no regrets, even since the reality of a shorter future became apparent. I think about dying and it scares me. I can't really talk to myself about it yet. When I think about it I feel really sad about leaving Mom alone. We are so close and I don't want to leave her. I am afraid of actually dying. It is easier to just keep going day by day so I will do that. Something changed when I decided that negative feelings were totally ineffective and negative energy was damaging. I have also come to realize that my spirit, my soul, all my creativity is not sick and that part of me will never die. Mom told me how much she has learned from me and how much she enjoys our time together. I have learned to live and enjoy every day, all the things we do and share together. I know that I can tell her anything and I feel so safe when she's around.

12/10/04 I want to fight harder and hope beyond hope that this lung disease stops progressing even as I know that it is unrealistic to expect this. I just can't die. I have too many dreams to achieve and I can't leave. I have my spirit strength. My soul is strong and I will eke out every second of this life.

Sometimes courage is hoping against hope.

1/6/05   I DO NOT want to die in a hospital. When I hear about hospice, it is all about dying and I don't want to be in that category. I feel very sad, like I've failed myself. I know I have no control over my illness and my body is failing. I try so hard to live each day to its fullest and that is really all I can do at this point.

2/25/05   I feel fortunate that design and creativity are what I love and am good at. This is something that doesn't take a lot of physical strength; it is a mental process and I can be in my bed in the dark and think of new knitting designs or LEGO building. I have been able to nurture my gifts. I have been able to learn to be confident and not let the world or my illness define me. Mom and Dad have been a big part of helping me see that. My life is far from "normal," yet it feels normal.

Life is made up of simple moments. There is happiness in that simplicity. Whatever our thoughts and fears, we come back to the moment and try to make each day the best it can be. In this way I am free to enjoy what I have because I can do what I want to do. It appears that for most people life is hectic and leaves little time to think, "Why am I doing this?" There are so many things that I wish I could have done in my life. I still hope somehow that I will live a long time and that my *dreams will come true. Maybe I'll be one of those medical miracles. I have a strong spirit and sense of self. It isn't easy growing up sick. It is hard to become more and more dependent. I never had the chance to be independent. I do have wonderful memories of my childhood before this illness overtook me. It is those days that I remember and yet I know I can never go back. I try not to wonder why this has happened to me since, even if I knew, it wouldn't change the now or make it better. All I can do is take what I have, no matter how little, and make it feel big because simple is grand. One moment can be a lifelong memory.*

7/18/05   I am still emotionally a disaster. I just can't deal with anything. It is too much and I feel very angry. Times of peace and joy and calm need to be treasured like gold because the future holds fewer rather than more such moments. I wonder about the future but try not to dwell on it. It is enough to just contemplate the here and now. I really want to cry out of complete frustration at times; there just aren't the words to express what I feel.

7/21/05   My feet are so swollen and they don't go down when I elevate them. They look like horrible, mutant feet. When I woke up last night I felt the elephant on my chest.

Sometimes courage is hoping against hope.

7/23/05   I was going to write a letter to Mom, just to tell her my feelings and let her know again how much I appreciate everything she does for me. I have a feeling of frustration and utter chaos, like everything is spiraling out of control. We just get deeper and deeper into the hole with no glimmer of light at the end. Any shining moment needs to be held onto for as long as possible. My focus is very short term and usually on what I want to do that day or the next. It is so hard to accept that life will only get harder, that my body will continue to deteriorate while I try to live around it.

8/1/05   I can't think of the future, it is too scary, so now is all I have and I try to make it the best I can. I can't think too much about how awful everything is because I don't want to waste the present. I have a feeling of unquiet and inner turmoil. I need some reassurance that we'll get through this and I'll never have to do it alone. I can't knit anymore because I can't see. I have no expectations or goals. The only goal is to make today become tomorrow.

8/28/05   I have a lot to write about. I was having a great time a couple days ago printing tiny flower pictures from the computer for the summer album when suddenly my back cracked really badly, the worst yet. For some reason I couldn't *hear either. Mom stayed with me until the medicine was delivered. I wish sometimes that I was small and could curl up in her lap and have her rock me. The pain resolved pretty quickly but the memory is scary and I have been having dreams of dying. They are so realistic. Life is very difficult and frustrating and it is all in my face right now. I guess we need to call hospice again. We made raspberry sherbet today and I got to lick the bowl. YUM! The big news is that Hurricane Katrina, a category 5, is heading right at New Orleans. I feel so bad about all the beautiful houses that will be destroyed. My writing is awful. I can't write what I feel anyway, I really just want to hide and cry; it is the easiest.*

Allison died on September 1, 2005. She left her parents a scrapbook of pictures from her life along with the following letter:

Dear Mom and Dad,

From day one I have been very lucky. I couldn't have picked better people for my parents. From the first times that I can remember you have been there for me. You have always encouraged me to believe in myself. You have given me the strength to believe that I can do anything that I want. Your love has always made me feel very safe. I can be myself all the time and never feel ashamed of who I am.

Sometimes courage is hoping against hope.

I have that ability because of you. I feel like I can face anything that comes along the road of life. Knowing that you are always there to love and support me has made me who I am today. I have so many wonderful memories of my life and childhood and they are of the simple times that I treasure most. We have always been a very happy little family and I wouldn't change any of it for the world!

Love always, your daughter,
Allison Elizabeth Caldwell

For a complete copy of Allison's journal as well as pictures of her and some of her creations, go to https://sites.google.com/site/allisonelizabethcaldwell.

Old age is the revenge of the ugly.

Forget safety.
Live where you fear to live.
Destroy your reputation.
Be notorious.

—Rumi

A derivative of our fear of death is our apprehension about the aging process. No aspect of our identities is more important than our date of birth. We segregate ourselves rigidly by age and, past a certain point in our twenties, share a fear of growing older. Our standards of physical beauty center on the good connective tissue that is the sole property of the young. As we look at the generation ahead of us or the one ahead of them, we are not usually encouraged by models of vigor and optimism.

Instead, we have lots of examples, usually including our own parents, of those who complain to the young about the physical consequences of growing older, as if they are surprised at their declining vitality and the diffuse aches that attend this process. Sharing the details of this diminishment is unlikely to entertain or draw us closer to those on whom we increasingly depend.

Birthdays come to have a more ominous meaning. Our cultural icons are, in general, those who possess the attributes of youth, and as we grow older we see fewer flattering reflections of ourselves in popular entertainment. In a vivid demonstration of our priorities, Americans spend roughly equivalent amounts on beauty products and cosmetic surgery as they do on public education.

From our earliest years, we are dissatisfied with our age. When we are children, we envy the freedom of adults to manage their own lives. As teenagers, especially, we chafe at the restrictions imposed on us as we seek autonomy in ways constructive and rebellious. Those of us who make the transition to adulthood usually, but not always, in our early twenties (have you seen the numbers of young people moving back home after college?) are still confronted with the tasks of earning a living and finding someone we imagine we will still love in our thirties and beyond. Somewhere in this phase of our lives, we begin to worry about aging.

A common perception of the elderly is that after retirement, they are no longer productive and are reduced to the role of consumers. A patient once described the process of aging this way: "It's like climbing a steep hill with failing strength while someone gradually adds rocks to your pack." The rocks are the losses we inevitably accrue as we age: our youth, our physical attractiveness, our health, those we love. The feeling that time passes more quickly as we age is not an illusion. As we grow older, each increment of time makes up a smaller percentage of our lives.

Absent in all this anxiety about aging is any sense that growing older might have its compensations. Freed of the urgent striving that marks our early adulthood, one would think that the elderly would have time to slow down and indulge the pleasures of mind and body that do not require the reflexes and strength that are gone forever. When I encounter older men who play golf, I am surprised at how often I hear stories of high school or college athletic triumphs. The theme is always the same: I wasn't always like this. Many of them have braces on their knees, damaged on fields distant in time, but the recollection is never bitter, always wistful, as if what they are now, old men trying to play an impossible game, is a rebuke to what they were once and might have been had they not been injured.

The subtext of these conversations is that the old have lost most of what we celebrate in this culture: energy, sexual adventure, a sense of possibilities, and the capacity to change the future. People instinctively prefer freedom of choice to the dead weight of habit and feelings of limited control. One of the major components of happiness is something to look forward to. As the distance between us and our life expectancy narrows, it is hard not to be discouraged, which explains the higher incidence of depression in this age group. In the words of Tennyson, "We are not now that strength that in old days moved earth and heaven." Was the implicit contract that governs our lives never properly explained to us? Perhaps when young, we didn't read the fine print: *If you are lucky enough to grow old, you will be stereotyped and marginalized by society, even by your own children. You will become slow of thought and movement and have to cope with unexplained pains. You will experience unspeakable losses that, finally, will include the loss of yourself. This is the bargain.* Perhaps if we had absorbed this part of the contract, we could see it through in good

51

humor and without complaint. Such an outcome would certainly be a relief to those who follow us.

Instead, we appear more inclined to act amazed and offended by what appears to be a rebuke to our sense of specialness. On his deathbed, the novelist William Saroyan supposedly said, "Everybody has got to die, but I always believed that an exception would be made in my case." Perhaps this unconscious assumption allows us to avoid what could otherwise be a morbid and immobilizing preoccupation with our mortality.

Whatever we believe about why we are here, we seem to take the most satisfaction from what we create. For most of us, this pleasure resides in our children and their children, those who carry our genetic material into the future. Few of us are lucky enough to have work that provides real creative satisfaction. Instead, for most jobs, little of what we do lives on after us and most of what we do can be done as well by others, so our presence is not missed for long.

Those of us who have chosen occupations in which we serve others—cocktail waitresses and psychiatrists, for example—hope that our efforts have improved the lives of a few of the people we have encountered. But it is not too modest to believe that the number of human beings who are really better for having encountered us is small.

Old age is the revenge of the ugly.

Because I am in a time of life when one contemplates one's impact on the world, I recently tried to estimate the percentage of those thousands of patients I have seen over forty-five years of work who are significantly better for having met me. My best guess is around 25 percent. Another 60 to 70 percent changed their lives little or not at all as a result of our conversations. I comfort myself that relatively few, therefore, are *worse* for having met me, but perhaps I am, even now, giving myself the benefit of the doubt. When I was in training, I told one of my supervisors that I would be interested to find out in ten years how a patient I had worked with in the hospital was doing. Only now do I understand his response: "Don't look back."

So, if we elect to take honest inventory of our lives as we near the end, perhaps modesty can coexist with satisfaction. It is given to few of us to leave anything behind that is memorable to others, much less permanent. Perhaps it is enough to have loved those we could, done as little harm as possible, and grown old with enough courage to give hope to (or at least amuse) the small audience who cared enough about us to pay attention.

In life beyond high school, no one gives you credit for effort.

The difference between what we do and what we are capable of doing would suffice to solve most of the world's problems.

—Mohandas Gandhi

Fear of humiliation is a modern-day analog of our fear of death. Likewise, a fear of failure often disguises itself as a drive for success. Surveys of business executives have disclosed a high incidence of the "impostor phenomenon," an apprehension among successful people that they are in danger of being unmasked as knowing less than they should. As we accumulate more education in any subject, we become aware of how little we know compared to how much information is available. Who among us can be said to have mastered physics or the science of human behavior? Why are people who are experts (if they are honest) loath to make generalizations or predictions? Are they just being modest, or do they realize more than the rest of us that the unknown, in every area of study, has always outweighed the fraction that we know?

An exception to the rule of professional modesty can be seen in those whose job it is to argue with each other and indoctrinate the rest of us in the areas of politics, philosophy, and religion. Here we find plenty of so-called experts prepared to display certainty in the absence of evidence-based knowledge. Fortunately for them, but unfortunately for everybody else, they are seldom held to account for their routinely inaccurate predictions.

Most of us are in agreement about the importance of education in the functioning of a civilized society. This idea is based on a belief that an informed population, armed with what is known about the world, will be in a better position to make rational decisions about what policies to pursue and whom to elect to pursue them. How far short of this ideal we currently are can be seen in the level of public discourse about things such as evolution, global warming, and whether a fertilized egg has achieved legal personhood. Where have we gone wrong when we elect people to public office who believe that the world is less than ten thousand years old and that human beings coexisted with the dinosaurs? It is but a short step from there to a conviction that the moon landing was faked and that the Twin Towers were demolished by the government. People impervious to knowledge have always been in our midst, but recently they have been granted access to public megaphones and legions of followers. Clearly our system of education has failed us in some critical areas.

School, in addition to transmitting information that we have agreed ought to be taught to young people, provides the laboratory in which we define ourselves socially. We derive our initial sense of where we fit in our complicated society from the way our contemporaries react to us. Only a few of us are comfortably "cool." Those who do not qualify must adopt alternative identities to sustain the hope that they will be able as adults to get their share of affection and worldly goods. In general, we are not taught the requirements for being happy and the traits to cultivate in ourselves and seek in others to satisfy our need for acceptance and closeness. This educational deficit is understandable because most adults haven't figured out workable answers to these important questions.

In life beyond high school, no one gives you credit for effort.

In the absence of reliable instruction or good role models, most adolescents fall back on peers to teach them how to succeed, especially in becoming attractive to the opposite sex. Most of the learning around these issues is through trial and error. And these frequently embarrassing experiences account for our lifetime fears that they will be repeated. Although the adult world encourages working hard for long-term goals and conformity to rules, adolescents prefer short-term pleasures and individuality. It is paradoxical that at a time of life when we think we will live forever, we often behave as if this were our last day on earth.

Then we enter that extended phase of adolescence called college. The news here is that testing of thousands of college students demonstrated not only that on average they spend about twelve to thirteen hours a week studying, but that 36 percent showed no gain in knowledge or critical thinking skills over the four years. So what *are* college students doing with that time? If you said partying, your critical thinking is intact. This reality speaks to more than confirming the old truth that "youth is wasted on the young." Such an emphasis on socializing also suggests that, well into their twenties, young people are, in general, learning what it means to be successful in a superficial and hedonistic environment.

Eventually, most of us have to grow up, get jobs, marry, and start making our way in a world that in general, values results over display. Although our fears about social inadequacy follow us into adulthood, we now have additional apprehension about making enough money to live comfortably and to attract a suitable marriage partner. Even in a liberated world, most women still hesitate if they hear that their date lives in his parents' basement.

This period of striving that marks the early (and middle) adulthood of most young people is when we become "sorted out" in the socioeconomic sense. Our educations are complete and our financial futures are, for the most part, predictable. Although we pay a lot of attention to outliers who strike it rich with novel ideas or financial acumen, make radical career changes, or implode because of addictions or character problems, most of us, though we may change jobs, end up in the same line of work in our fifties that we started in our twenties. Whether this is good or bad news depends on how much you like your job. Most people don't derive a lot of "psychological income" from their work and see it primarily as a routine activity that feeds their families and allows them to pursue more enjoyable activities in their free time.

In life beyond high school, no one gives you credit for effort.

In our personal lives, meanwhile, a lot of us are engaged in paying for our mistakes—mostly errors we recognize in our middle age that we made when we were young. Prominent among these mistakes is frequently your choice of life partner, which, for at least half of us, takes the form of divorce from a person with whom we have children. This unhappy fact is the source of a new set of fears about the consequences of divorce and the prospects for companionship in the future. Divorced or not, life in middle age is usually extremely complicated, with simultaneous responsibilities to our kids and to our aging parents.

Finally, after we survive all that, we are eligible to start coping with our own old age. If we retire from work, we frequently face a loss of identity no matter how onerous our jobs seemed at the time we were doing them. We can no longer avoid the reality that the time we have left is limited and must face the gap between our youthful aspirations and our actual lives. No matter our success or lack of it (and who can make that judgment?), most of us feel some regret and uncertainty about whether we have played the hands we were dealt with enough skill and effort. Did we choose the right work? Could we have been better at it? Did we spend enough time with our children who now need us hardly at all?

We all have difficulty envisioning a world in which we do not partake even as we receive regular evidence of our replaceability. We cherish a sense of specialness while time with its milestones reminds us of our mortality. We fear extinction and wonder at the meaning of it all—all the striving, all the relationships, all the pain. What difference has it made? What difference have *we* made? Religion may answer some of these questions for some people, but it poses another. Have we met our obligations to our faith?

Fear lurks behind perfectionism.

We are more often frightened than hurt; and
we suffer more from imagination than from reality.
—Seneca the Elder

Of all the burdens we inflict on ourselves and those around us, perfectionism is among the weightiest. Each of us has experienced the products and services of those with an indifference to quality: toys that break on first use, unreliable and expensive car repairs, incorrect orders at restaurants, planes that don't run on time, hours on the phone waiting for tech support, bungled police investigations. The list of human failures of competence is long.

To combat these inefficiencies, businesses adopt all manner of quality control approaches to construct a society in which things work most of the time. "Zero defects" is an ideal frequently sought but seldom achieved. Although this process of intolerance for error makes for a reasonably efficient business environment, it has some critical disadvantages when applied to the murky area of human relationships. For example, a Yale law professor, in her book *Battle Hymn of the Tiger Mother*, promotes the idea that raising successful kids requires that parents make all the decisions about how their children spend their time: basically either studying or practicing music. Because the secret to academic or musical success is "tenacious practice, practice, practice," sleepovers, play dates, school plays, TV, and computer games are not permitted. Nor is the child allowed to get any grade below A. The justification for this regime is that "children on their own never want to work, which is why it is crucial to override their preferences." If the child resists this program of "rote repetition," it is okay to "excoriate, punish and shame the child." The author tells one anecdote about the horrified reaction of Western parents at a dinner party when she apparently bragged about calling her daughter "garbage."

Even allowing for some exaggeration on the part of an author selling a book, this material is challenging for parents wanting the best for their kids. We are forced to reflect on issues such as what constitutes success in this society and what values we want to transmit to our children. The debate takes place against a background of concern about narcissism and a sense of entitlement that, fairly or unfairly, are seen as implicit cultural values in twenty-first-century America. The book in question defines success solely in terms of individual achievement, with little attempt to conceal the mother's contempt for the poorly parented "losers" with whom her children are competing.

One would be hard-pressed to find a better example of fear as a motivator than the parenting style advocated by someone who argues that lectures, insults, and intimidation are the essence of successful parenting. Such an approach manifests a deeply pessimistic view of human nature that supposes that our children and, by extension, the rest of us are fundamentally lazy and driven by uncontrolled desires for pleasure. Therefore, we must be forced by some external source—parents, religion, government—to conform to a rigid set of rules that will make us better, or at least more tractable, people. Such an assumption requires many constraints and prohibitions ("Thou shalt not"), with fear as the basic enforcement mechanism. One need only observe life in a theocratic society such as

Iran or Afghanistan under the Taliban to get a taste of how that idea works.

Because everyone concedes that we must have rules to regulate our lives together, we must also have penalties for breaking these rules. This is the theory upon which our justice system rests. But our efforts should lie in striking a balance between positive and negative consequences. If you believe that most people have a conscience and a sense of obligation to each other, you are likely to behave (and expect others to behave) in a different way than if you believe that we are motivated primarily by our own self-interest and are restrained from taking advantage of others only by a system of punitive law.

Perhaps 1 percent of the population, however, are unrestrained by conscience and spend their lives exploiting their fellow citizens. These people are the sociopaths against whom we must protect ourselves; their incidence in prison populations is about 25 percent. They respond only to negative consequences and are therefore dangerous to the people around them. Unfortunately, their relentless pursuit of their own self-interest combined with their glib and exploitive personalities sometimes cause them to rise to the top in political and business pursuits. Their incidence among successful executives and politicians has been estimated at 4 percent.

Fear lurks behind perfectionism.

Most of our fears about sociopathic behavior focus on our personal apprehensions. People routinely overestimate the prevalence of crime and have exaggerated fears of being victimized. Entire cable channels are devoted to crime stories. Our fear of violence drives the debate about the need for every citizen to bear arms even in churches and on college campuses, even though our chances of needing to defend ourselves are vanishingly small.

The signal defect in self-absorbed personality disorders such as narcissism and sociopathy is an absence of empathy. Most people's concerns about criminal behavior are directed at individual acts of violence. What we should really wish to discern are instances in which those in power, who have the ability to affect the lives of millions, routinely display deficits in their ability to hear heartbeats other than their own. We are entertained by the hypocrisies of politicians, movie stars, and persons of wealth, especially when their offenses involve sexual infidelity. Why is it that the offenders, when exposed, so frequently turn out to be those who have been judgmental about the transgressions or sexual lives of others? Does a connection exist between a public promulgation of "family values" and a private decision to live differently?

Of all the ways we betray ourselves and the people around us, infidelity is one of the most common and consequential. And much of it is driven by fear: fear of the aging process with its implacable loss of physical attractiveness, fear that we have not in our lives had our share of novel sex, fear that others may be enjoying themselves more than we are. The Hollywood portrayal of relationships is bound to leave many with a feeling that they have lived inhibited lives with few opportunities to satisfy their sexual desires. Sex sells, so we are bombarded with images of youth and beauty that seem tantalizingly out of reach for most of us.

We are not really taught by our parents or the culture that really good sex occurs in the context of a relationship in which the participants care about themselves and each other equally. Instead, we are frightened with prohibitions, religious and otherwise, that only make the forbidden fruit of extramarital relationships seem more exciting. As Adam and Eve could not resist partaking of the knowledge of good and evil, so we find ways to ruin our lives on the altar of infidelity. Some even argue that people, like most animals, are not wired for monogamy. Television shows celebrate polygamy, though it exists as a gender-specific institution of one man and multiple wives, which raises questions about the role of male entitlement. And we are faced with the question behind all moral judgments: Who, if anyone, is being hurt? If the wives, as they claim, are happy with the bargain and have been able to foreswear jealousy, what is the harm in *any* alternative definition of what constitutes a relationship? Perhaps such arrangements are simply another symptom, such as the high divorce rate, of the decline in conventional marriage?

And yet most of us cling to the ideal of monogamous commitments even though half of our first lunges at matrimony do not endure. The ideal of one other person loving us as we are, coming home to us every night, being willing to have children with us, and consenting to grow old together appears to have a permanent hold on our dreams. So we seek such a person from the time we are young without knowing precisely who we are looking for. That the process is prone to mistakes, heartbreak, and second effort is daunting yet inevitable. We know we are born alone and will die alone, but aloneness between these events is intolerable and so we continue to seek each other out in what I like to call "the search for the perfect stranger." A few are lucky enough to find that person; the rest stop at nothing in the effort. If only we had a better idea of who we are looking for, we might have a better chance of preparing ourselves to find him or her and answer the question that drives us: *Can two imperfect people form a perfect relationship that will inspire them to forsake all others, not as an obligation, but as a gift?*

Courage is not a feeling; it is a habit.

To sin by silence when they should protest
makes cowards of us all.

—Abraham Lincoln

Fear is a disorienting emotion. It can freeze us or impel us toward frantic, irrational action. When we are afraid, thinking clearly about cause and effect is difficult. The "fight or flight" reaction is a product of a surge of adrenalin that prevents thoughtful reflection. If fear becomes chronic, we call it anxiety, an emotional disability that is less acute than fear itself (except during a panic attack). We exist in a more or less constant state of worry and unease, and will do anything to avoid situations that trigger or enhance the anxiety. Such avoidance behavior leads paradoxically to the cardinal rule of anxiety: Attempts to evade our fears make them worse.

The converse is also true: *The only way to overcome fear is to confront it.* This response requires determination because the process of fear reduction is slow. For example, many years ago, I had a fear of heights that I seldom had occasion to challenge. But when I chose a life as a soldier, the Army required that I learn how to jump out of airplanes. With the help of my fellow soldiers, most of whom were also afraid of this unnatural pursuit, I managed to throw myself from an airplane and was gratified to find that, one, the parachute opened as planned, two, the landing I had practiced did not result in injury, and three, the view on the way down was spectacular. The second time I jumped I was still afraid but slightly less so. By the tenth jump I was enjoying the experience, and by the twentieth I was seeking out opportunities to jump and had started teaching others how to do it. (It's not that complicated.) This process, called *desensitization*, is a model for coping with all sorts of phobias, from a fear of escalators to crowds to traveling through tunnels.

Facing fear as a way to diminish it is not a novel idea,

though it appears to be to those who have never tried it. Avoidance, after all, requires much less effort and does provide short-term anxiety relief.

A larger lesson is implied in the decision to confront our fears: What does it mean to live a small life as opposed to an expansive one, that is, a life that benefits others? Our society emphasizes material success. We imagine that the primary constraint upon our choices is a lack of money, that if we had lots of it we could "live large" with big houses, expensive cars, and exotic travel—all the trappings that separate the rich from the rest of us. We seldom measure our accomplishments by our influence on others. Most of us have a sense of how important we are to those who love us: our parents, our spouses, our children. The trust they repose in us is an obligation that we take seriously. When we think of the larger world, few of us believe that what we do, or fail to do, has much impact on other people. We stop at red lights to avoid collisions, but few of us give anything to the homeless person who approaches our car while we're waiting for the light to change. Some of us even tell him to "get a job." He is not a part of our world and we feel no responsibility for him.

We argue with each other about what we should do collectively to help those who, for whatever reason, have not succeeded in their efforts to pay their own way. Do the elderly deserve to have income support from the rest of us? Is housing for the indigent a social obligation? What of health care for children whose parents cannot afford it? The answers to these questions are a larger variation of the individual decisions we make about whether to be involved with the lives of others, not simply because there is an unfilled need but because to be so involved is a measure of the size and value of our own lives.

Fear plays a role in these policy decisions because at some level we know that except for certain accidental factors—the kind of family we were born into, our ability to learn, the education our parents could afford, the demand for the services we provide, the stability of the company we work for—we too could be homeless or otherwise in need. One response to such a realization is to confuse our good fortune with some virtue we possess, such as our capacity for hard work. If we can believe that this quality is what accounts for our success, we can blame those less fortunate for their own failure, hence the judgment that they have brought misfortune on themselves through laziness or substance abuse and are not deserving of our help, either individually or through our government.

This habit of averting our eyes from hardship works only until we experience our own losses and calamities. When the tornado strikes our street, when someone close to us dies, when we are reminded of the fragility of all we have and all we love, we are finally humbled. We realize, as if for the first time, that we live in a universe where rewards and punishments are, in fact, not allocated by merit. Nothing is odder than survivors of a plane crash who attribute their luck to their faith: "I prayed and God saved me," as if the unanswered prayers of the dead somehow never reached God's ears. In a movie portrayal of a therapy group for bereaved parents, one of the mothers seeks comfort in a familiar formulation: "God needed another angel, so he took our daughter." Another mother asks, "If he needed an angel, why didn't he just make one? He's God, after all."

Such mysteries puzzle and terrify us. What is required to respond bravely to the evident fact that we have so little control over what happens to us? First we must work our way through the pointless questions before we can develop even tentative answers to the ones that lead somewhere. "Why me?" is a familiar response to unanticipated catastrophe. The answer, heartless in its simplicity, is "Why not you?" A more productive question is: "What do I do now?" The truth is that *as long as we live, we are never out of choices*. If we can convince ourselves of this truth, we can work our way through the natural self-pity we all experience when beset by life's plentiful injustices. We need to find a realistic place between the narcissistic illusion that we will be spared the experience of watching our best hopes collapse and the belief that life is meaningless if we cannot control it. If we can find such a middle ground, we will not relinquish the fight.

Beware of ideas on which we all agree.

We promise according to our hopes;
we fulfill according to our fears.
—La Rouchefoucauld

No shared feelings are more firmly embedded in American culture than the admiration and gratitude that we feel toward the young men and women who have served in our most recent wars. Their sacrifices are celebrated at every opportunity, and stories about our "wounded warriors" and their families are a staple of the nightly news. Our great national spectacles—sporting events, holidays—become occasions for patriotic celebration and remembrance, rife with clichés (such as "Freedom isn't free") designed to reassure us that, while we personally have not chosen to sacrifice anything during wartime, we at least appreciate those who have made the choice to do so. They stand in their camouflage uniforms often looking a little mystified at the applause.

The reflexive impulse to treat our troops as heroes serves an important purpose apart from relieving our guilt at having done nothing ourselves. The war in Iraq, no less than other wars, involved the morally ambiguous process of killing large numbers of people who posed no threat to us. Because the instruments of destruction were our sons and daughters, we find it hard to take responsibility for asking this of them without regret and self-examination. Ignoring our misjudgments and redoubling our admiration for the young people who risked everything on our behalf are far easier.

When the public repudiated the war of my generation, the veterans of Vietnam found themselves criticized or overlooked as unwelcome reminders of a colossal and expensive national blunder. Ironically, we did not learn from this experience that going to war when we are not threatened is an error. All we understood from Vietnam was that blaming our soldiers for the mistakes of our leaders was unjust.

And so the pendulum has now swung toward lionizing

everyone in uniform, thanking them for their service when they stride through airports like the Roman legionnaires of old, representatives of the American empire that has come to imagine that it can impose its will on the world by the strength of its armed forces rather than the force of its ideas.

The "Support our troops" bumper magnets that blossomed as the invasion of Iraq commenced could have just as well read "My country, right or wrong!" We had been attacked and now we were attacking back. Afghanistan, which is where the terrorists who struck us lived, became secondary to what our national leadership declared a "target-rich environment" for our tanks and cruise missiles: Iraq. Eight years, one trillion dollars, and forty-five hundred American lives later, we have finally left. Are we safer now? More free? No, but we appreciate all that those one million Americans who served there have done. As long as we honor them, no one need reflect or apologize or be held accountable.

Apart from the decisions that led to the war itself, there were, as there are in all wars, things to apologize for. The pictures of the mistreatment of prisoners at Abu Ghraib appeared to have only a passing impact on the conscience of most Americans. The muted response was reminiscent of our reaction in 1970 to the images of the

Beware of ideas on which we all agree.

My Lai massacre in the pages of *Life* magazine. When U.S. Marines killed twenty-four unarmed civilians in the town of Haditha in 2005 or American contractors killed seventeen in a busy square in Baghdad in 2007, little note was taken or responsibility required. Most estimates put the overall Iraqi civilian death toll at more than one hundred thousand. Make what you will of the fact that we keep an accurate count of only our own deaths.

An Iraqi family is killed at a U.S. checkpoint as they are rushing a child to a hospital. These things happen in the "fog of war." The soldiers involved, fearing suicide bombers, had to protect themselves when the car didn't stop. Listen to the words of a state department official working on reconstruction in Iraq. "We tried to convince them we were the good guys and that we'd gotten rid of Saddam, but given all the killings that had happened, that never hung together." He recalled an occasion when he distributed fruit trees to farmers in a rural area. One refused to accept the seedling and spat on the ground. His son had been killed accidentally by U.S. forces, the farmer said, "and you're giving me a fruit tree?"

And so we venerate those who put themselves in fear-inducing situations on our behalf and did whatever they could to survive. Most of them are neither heroes nor killers, just patriotic people volunteering to hazard themselves for reasons that to them seemed good at the time. Can we deal with our fears in some way that does not involve the use of bullets or high explosives? Can we celebrate those willing to take risks while creating alternative ways for young people to serve their country that are less costly to them and to others in distant places who love their children in the same way that we love ours?

❦

We were sitting down to Christmas Eve dinner at the 7th Surgical Hospital, Blackhorse Basecamp, Republic of Vietnam. The year was 1968. It was a quiet night in the war, and the doctors and nurses were looking forward to an evening eating turkey, exchanging presents, and longing to be elsewhere.

The bad news came, as it always did, from the night radio operator, whispering in the ear of the hospital commander. "Ladies and gentlemen," the colonel said, "we have casualties coming in."

We had heard these words before. The lights were turned on at the helicopter landing pad in anticipation of the medevac Hueys with their cargoes of wounded soldiers. It was always hard to see those young men, bodies shattered, wearing the stunned looks of the suddenly old.

But most of us had become used to it, and we waited for wounded soldiers.

Not this time. Tonight the harvest of the war was children. They came to us, two or three to a litter, in field ambulances, from the nearby town of Xuan Loc. They had been in a holiday crowd, and an adult had decided to set off a colorful smoke grenade of the sort the Army used to mark helicopter landing zones. These were harmless and gave off red, green, or white smoke.

The children must have gathered closely to watch. A pity that the man could not read the lettering on the canister: "White Phosphorus." The grunts called it "Willie Peter" and used it to mark positions for air strikes. First it exploded into a fine powder that stuck to everything it touched. Then it burned.

These children were burning. Except for the very young, they, like the wounded men we were used to seeing, did not cry out. We shouted for cupric chloride to soak the wounds; water was useless against the phosphorus. Gallons of the blue liquid were hurriedly splashed on the small bodies. Two of the children had been blinded; several, we could tell, were burned too extensively to survive.

As I worked through that night, I thought of my own children far away. The parents of these kids were not allowed on the base for security reasons, so for now the children were ours. We couldn't get a helicopter to evacuate the most badly burned because no American had been injured. It was an accident, we told ourselves, no fault of ours or our soldiers. But like most of the misery inflicted on the Vietnamese, intentional and incidental, that grenade was made in the USA. By dawn, five of the children were dead. The rest will bear the scars of that Christmas Eve for the rest of their lives. As will I.

There is no humor in heaven.

The secret source of humor itself
is not joy, but sorrow.
—Mark Twain

Example: If you don't go to your friends' funerals, you can't expect them to come to yours.

Freud conceived the existence of psychological "defense mechanisms," unconscious strategies we use to cope with reality and to maintain our self-image. Some of these efforts are pathological, such as denial or delusions. Others are "mature," such as altruism, anticipation, and humor (though it must be said that a lot of what passes for funny is pretty immature). The ability to laugh, especially at ourselves, has been shown to have beneficial effects on both physical and mental health. Years ago, Norman Cousins wrote a book about curing a mysterious and persistent illness by watching Marx brothers movies. I must admit, however, that I must endorse the following sentiment from a get-well card: *Anyone who thinks that laughter is the best medicine has apparently never had morphine.* A popular bumper sticker on cars years ago read *Hugs are better than drugs.* I have been known to put post-it notes on such vehicles in parking lots with the question, *Have you tried both?*

People in extremely fear-inducing situations—combat, for example—frequently use humor as a defense. In Vietnam, the people who regularly took the greatest risks were the Long Range Reconnaissance Patrols ("Lurps"), who were often left in small numbers for days at a time to perform such tasks as count and harass enemy troops and vehicles coming down the Ho Chi Minh trail. Their compound at Bien Hoa was marked by the following sign: "12th LRRP." Below was a reminder to the rest of us: "No war stories please."

Everything can be a source of humor: *Moses comes down from the mountain and says to his followers, "There's good news and there's bad news. The good news is that I got Him down to ten. The bad news is that adultery stays in."*

There is no humor in heaven.

❦

In 1982, Air Florida Flight 90 crashed into the Potomac River on takeoff, leaving only five survivors. The next day, a Washington disc jockey called the Air Florida ticket office from his program to ask the fare from National Airport to the 14th Street bridge. Even 9/11, which was widely predicted to put an end to humor and irony, produced this: *A fireman goes home on 9/11 and tells his wife about his day. "My buddy, Stan, and I were running toward one tower after the other one fell, but then Stan got hit by a jumper so I stopped to help him. Thirty seconds later, the north tower collapsed. If Stan didn't get hit, we both would have been goners!" The fireman's wife turns to him and says, "Is this going to be a long story?"*

Or: *Have you heard that American Airlines now has flights from Boston directly to your office in New York?*

See what I mean? If we're willing to tolerate some tastelessness, there's little that cannot be lampooned. Our greatest insecurities are fair game. *A man and his wife are in marriage counseling. He says, "One thing that bothers me is that you never tell me when you have an orgasm." She replies, "You're usually not there."*

What are we doing when we laugh at the human condition (even at its most tragic) and thereby at ourselves? *A woman says to her psychiatrist, "Oh doctor, please kiss me. He replies, "That would be unethical. I shouldn't even be lying on this couch with you."*

In our jokes, we are acknowledging the simultaneous absurdity and infinite value of our lives. Or, as one writer put it, "things may be critical but they need not be serious." The passage of time enables us to find humor in the most terrible events: *Everyone needs to stop making Holocaust jokes. Can you nazi how hurtful they are?*

Because the judgment about what is funny is so subjective, any attempt at humor has an implied risk. (This is why I put the jokes in *italics*.) Humor is often used as a weapon to degrade or humiliate others, so there is a fine line to observe. In general, jokes that play into stereotypes or target the powerless are not funny. Given the differences in our senses of humor and the virtual absence of it in some people, we are all in danger of giving offense, as I have doubtless done already. Yet it is worth seeing laughter as a courageous and curative act and one of our best defenses against the fate that awaits us all.

The essence of humor is surprise. Most of us can only imagine the courage required to stand in front of an audience with the sole purpose of making them laugh. When Woody Allen said, "I don't want to achieve immortality through my work. I want to achieve it by not dying," he was speaking to a persistent fantasy shared by many of us (as he was when he described himself as "always putting my ex-wife under a pedestal"). If we can laugh in the face of our mistakes and our mortality, we can perhaps bring ourselves to tolerate our existential anxiety and enjoy whatever time we have been given.

People with mental illness customarily lose their sense of humor. Years ago, I performed a psychiatric evaluation on an accused murderer in prison. Attempting to establish rapport, I asked him, "What shall I call you?" He responded unsmilingly, "Why don't you call me a cab and let's get the hell out of here." To this day, I am not sure whether he was exhibiting a symptom called concrete thinking or a sarcastic wit. People who are ill or neurotic are prone to the use of acting out or repression as a mechanism to cope with anxiety rather than the more adaptive defense that humor represents.

It has been said, "You don't have a sense of humor; it has you." Being able to see serious matters from a humorous perspective is a habit developed over years of practice. One only needs to watch amateurs doing stand-up comedy to see how difficult it is to make others laugh. Your family may think you're funny, but getting a roomful of strangers to agree is hard. If it is true that without sorrow there is no humor, comedy will have little place in heaven. Perhaps things will be less boring elsewhere.

A beggar walks up to a man on the street and says, "Can I have a dollar for a sandwich?" The man says, "I don't know, let me see the sandwich."

12

Determination in the pursuit of folly is the indulgence of fools.

We are more afraid of losing what we have than not getting what we want.

—A well-researched rule of life

The most lethal combination of character traits, for men and nations, turns out to be arrogance allied to ignorance. Knowledge helps us manage fear. Stupidity thrives in the absence of curiosity and is frequently disguised by ambition and a relentless perseverance that can be a virtue only when the path chosen is informed and comports with reality. Passion can ennoble or destroy us, depending on the wisdom that directs it.

We live at the mercy of fools; they are everywhere. Their defining characteristics—a lack of comprehension, judgment, or common sense—are on frequent display among both our political representatives and the people who elect them. They exhibit an inability or unwillingness to learn from experience, and their grasp of basic information is frequently shaky.

Consider this account of Paul Revere's Ride from a leading politician on a trip to Boston: "He who warned the British that they weren't going to be taking away our arms by ringing those bells and making sure as he was riding his horse through town to send those warning shots and bells that we were gonna be secure and we were gonna be free." What does such a statement say about this person's understanding of American history? When we hear people holding forth on the Constitution who grasp little of its meaning, when they extol the founding fathers as fundamentalist Christians, when they assert that the Civil War was not fought over slavery, more is revealed than an imperfect education.

A further indicator of foolishness is a contempt or lack of understanding of the *scientific method*, that objective mode of inquiry that for four hundred years has been our best means of understanding our world. This approach to new knowledge requires systematic observation, measurement, and experiment, and the formulation, testing, and modification of hypotheses. The scientific method forswears evidence-free argument and has proven the only reliable escape from the magical thinking that preceded it. When contention is based instead on prejudice or religious belief, we have wandered into the realm of fools. When people deny the role of humans in climate change or dismiss evolution as "a theory" to be taught to our children alongside creationism, they are revealing a misperception of, even disdain for, reality that is both uninformed and dangerous.

When our understanding of the world is largely defined by an ancient text, be it the Bible or the Koran, we have left the pursuit of testable hypotheses and the experimental method and entered the area where our primary source of argument in all areas is clouded by a set of unverifiable beliefs. At a time when an unacceptable percentage of our workforce is unemployed, for example, many in our governments are preoccupied with issues that flow from religious convictions about when life begins. In a sense, this is a break with reality of the sort that afflicts people struggling with psychotic thinking. A hallmark of psychosis is delusional thought that is the product of false beliefs. And so it is with government when it is preoccupied with faith-based arguments at moments that call for reality-based solutions.

When the image of ourselves does not comport with the truth of our actions, we are also prone to terrible mistakes. For example, Americans like to see themselves as a peace-loving people who fight with others only when we or our core values are threatened. Yet we look back upon seventy years of more or less continual engagement in war. This attempt to bend the world to our needs and desires has had a spotty record of success and has cost us dearly. Although the analogy is imperfect, if we were as aggressive in our personal lives as we have been as a nation, we would likely be in jail. Once again, we confront the disconnect between reality and ideology. If we fight for "freedom," can we not ask ourselves how much freer we are than when we went to war in Vietnam or Iraq? Are we really learning from experience?

Primitive man lived in an atmosphere of fear. Faced with continual threats to his life by other, larger animals and confronted with a natural world he could not explain, he developed survival instincts that were adaptive at the time. For protection, he adopted kinship groups that expanded into larger communities that were more efficient at hunting, agriculture, and self-defense. It is only when these groups began to fight with each other over territory or food that the seeds of war were planted. As the weapons used became more destructive, we "progressed" to a situation in which all human life was threatened by differences among nation-states over ideologies concerning how best to organize society, politically and economically. We survived forty years of nuclear stand-off in the twentieth century. When the Communist side of the conflict crumbled economically, there was a brief hope that we might begin to settle differences without the threat of war. Soon, though, in the face of an atrocity by a relatively small group of religious fanatics, we declared ourselves at war again and have behaved in the ensuing ten years as if our entire way of life were threatened by people willing to blow themselves up.

It can be argued that if a nation spends 6 percent of its gross national product ($24 billion) each year on the military, it will find a way to use these forces. I think that the causes for our present martial (not to be confused with marital) adventures lie deeper in our vulnerability to fear and the cohesiveness that fear provides. In a society that contains many different conceptions of how we should be organized, how we should educate our children, how we treat the poor, how our considerable resources should be expended, we can all agree on few things. Our wars are presumably subject to debate as well, but a certainty among nearly all of us is that the highest calling, deserving of universal respect and adulation, is the role of soldier. The flag waving and parades that are routine accompaniments of our national holidays are orgies of patriotism that draw us together in a celebration of our presumed American exceptionalism. It is hard to imagine, by contrast, a similar acknowledgment of Peace Corps volunteers.

Perhaps this unifying effect of war is inevitable. We all are brought together by perceived threats. But this unity has its drawbacks. We too easily become attached to the primitive idea that the best way to live in an uncertain and dangerous world is to project our military power wherever we feel threatened. Conflict is so much more interesting than negotiation, which is why violence plays such a large role in our entertainment industry. Violence carries with it the illusion of control: If we are strong enough, no one can harm us and we will always have our way. If this were a correct analysis of how the world works, we would fear nothing. Violence is also commonly presented as the shortest path to peace. If that were true, we would have been at peace for some time now. In fact, it appears to be the preparation, even enthusiasm, for war that makes us so quick to engage in it. The adage applies: "If your only tool is a hammer, every problem looks like a nail."

So here's the argument: We have plenty of stupidity to go around. When this trait finds expression in a philosophy of government that extols selfishness and the use of force to get our way in the world, we are all in danger. We must eventually reject this kind of response to anxiety and uncertainty, not simply because it is morally wrong but because it doesn't work. (The same might be said of that other popular form of institutionalized vengeance, the death penalty.) The country has endured threats to its existence in the past without wavering on the rights of all human beings and a determination to act within the laws we have established. Our willingness to suspend these rights, even to torture people as a matter of national policy, is a recent phenomenon related to the fears that flowed from a horrifying national catastrophe. When these fears became politically useful, they were fanned by people who benefited from a frightened constituency. We were reflexively convinced that two wars were justified and that, in fact, these conflicts were just the beginning of a "long twilight struggle" with religious fanatics who derive their power from their ability to terrorize us. Over the last ten years, we have lost and taken many lives and spent more than we can afford in the service of our anxiety. Whether we have learned anything in return remains to be seen.

Courage can be taught only by example.

And what he greatly thought he nobly dared.

—Homer

After we have defined courage as *a choice to confront our fears,* we wonder how to both express and teach this virtue to our children. The lecture method will not work here, and our schools have little room in their curricula to teach virtue (even if they knew how). No matter how much we wish to be safe, life gives us many opportunities to be brave, if only in the ways we age, experience loss, treat each other, and face our mortality.

Of all the forms of courage that we celebrate, physical courage is the easiest to recognize, which is why we make heroes of our athletes. The kind of fortitude required to endure pain and face injury while displaying skill on the playing field is easy to observe and universally admired. Athletics provide our most reliable meritocracy. Although in most human endeavors we can pretend to be something we are not, the ability to play a game well cannot be faked. People who themselves cannot hit a ball or make a tackle nevertheless can become expert at discerning the skill or lack of it of those who do such things for a living. "Toughness," a synonym for physical courage, is an easily recognizable trait, especially in contact sports, for those who pursue the remorseless goal of victory. Sports also emphasize what one does right now, overshadowing past accomplishment. Each game is a new beginning with a requirement to perform again with the knowledge that your job is always at risk and that others, equally talented, are eager to take your place. Imagine having that pressure in *your* job.

However athletic we may be, we soon learn that our chances of earning a living playing a game are remote because too many others are better. We need to find some other way to express courage in our lives. The most widely recognized form of courage is again physical and consists of some form of military heroism. An entire graduated system of valor awards has been established to recognize courage in battle—above the risk that all soldiers assume by their willingness just to be there. Unfortunately, to bring this system to bear we require a war. Although it is not often spoken of, part of the appeal of war is that it serves as a stage on which courage is tested and rewarded. In this sense, military service has been a traditional rite of passage for men, which explains, for example, some of the enthusiasm that has traditionally marked the onset of our military adventures, from the Civil War to Iraq. Only in retrospect do we seem to appreciate the costs of these enterprises.

The award of medals for valor in combat is a notoriously flawed process involving witness descriptions, the military's need for heroes, and even the occasional requirement for a cover-up. War story: As a flight surgeon in Vietnam, part of my assignment was to provide medical services to the helicopter unit that was attached to our regiment. An officer in this unit was noted for his recklessness as well as his relentless womanizing. One day he was flying his helicopter back from Saigon with his current girlfriend on board; she was a civilian employee for a relief agency. He heard over the radio that his unit was in contact with the enemy. Against policy, he diverted to the area and, as he flew over, he ordered his door gunner to drop a white phosphorous grenade as a marker for an airstrike. The door gunner pulled the pin on the grenade before discovering that the other side of the aircraft would be better placed to drop it on the target. He handed the grenade across the helicopter to the crew chief, and as he did so, the spoon flew off, activating the timer. The crew chief threw it out the door, but as it left his hand it exploded, killing him and sending burning white phosphorous powder back into the helicopter. The pilot got some on the back of his neck, and his girlfriend, who was wearing flip-flops, got some on her feet. I met the helicopter as it arrived at the 93rd Evacuation Hospital and was enlisted in the uncomfortable task of explaining to medics in the receiving area why a female civilian had just been injured in a combat operation. Careers were at stake here, and the hospital commander was persuaded to omit this casualty from his records. The pilot received a Purple Heart and a Distinguished Flying Cross; the brave but unlucky crew chief, thanks to an enhanced description of his accidental death, received the Congressional Medal of Honor. Thus, sometimes, are heroes created. (See also Silver Star citation for Cpl. Pat Tillman, killed by his own unit in Afghanistan.)

Here is the larger point: War is so terrible in its dehumanization and destruction that it has no justification apart from national survival. When we engage in war in

Courage can be taught only by example.

the absence of such an imperative, a lot of effort is directed at its one redeeming feature: It elicits acts of courage from some of those who participate. If we pay enough attention to these actions, we can distract ourselves from the corrosive impact on us and our values that unjust or unnecessary wars exact. Hence the need to characterize as heroic all of our soldiers, especially those who died. We cannot acknowledge that they died in vain without reflecting the fact that, in a democracy, we were complicit in allowing the war in the first place. So we send our young off to kill and die while praising their sacrifices and extolling their heroism to obscure the futility of what we have asked them to do. Somehow our gratitude ("Thank you for your service") doesn't quite cover the true costs of our mistake.

Missing in our search for heroes outside ourselves is any sense that we have an obligation to exhibit courage in our own lives. Recently, in a California seaside community, fire and rescue personnel watched a man drown about one hundred yards offshore because they were following a policy of "no water rescues" that had been imposed by the town in response to budgetary constraints. No one, not any of the firemen, not one of the onlookers, went into the water to save this man, though they described themselves later as "frustrated" by a *rule* that apparently overcame whatever moral obligation they might have felt to this drowning man.

As long as we imagine that bravery requires some physical challenge, we see few opportunities to exhibit it in the relatively safe world we inhabit. A television show called *What Would You Do?* depicts people's reactions to simulated situations such as a woman being harassed by her boyfriend and a child being berated by a parent. You will not be surprised to hear that most people avoid involvement. In real life, hearing that those in distress were ignored by passersby is commonplace. The occasional people who respond helpfully are often asked to explain why they did what few others seem prepared to do. They are customarily at a loss to explain their reaction. What distinguishes this tiny minority appears to be a well-developed intolerance for injustice combined with a sense of responsibility for a fellow human being whom they do not know.

Like any virtue, courage (a form of kindness, after all) is not randomly distributed in the population. In my lifetime, the struggle for civil rights stands out as an example of this fact. Some people gave their lives for the idea of equality before the law; others loosed police dogs and fire hoses to defend injustice; most of us stayed home.

14

Nothing prepares us for the terrible risk of intimacy.

*The answer is to show up anyway, stammering and weeping,
and do the thing or stay in the place that engenders the fear.*

—Susan Cheever

Of all the tasks we set for ourselves, the choice of the person with whom we expect to spend the rest of our life is the most important and carries with it our slender and diluted hope for immortality (excepting eternity in heaven). That we are poor at making this choice is evident in the routine failures of marriage that dot the landscape. If giving our heart to another is such an important undertaking, why do we not train our young to recognize and develop those traits of character that make for satisfying and enduring relationships?

Think what you knew as a teenager, the time when you began to learn to engage in the great human experiment that you hoped would result in a lasting intimacy with another human being. Think what models you had of adults who had solved this problem in their lives. Think of what the popular culture taught you about who was hot and who was not. How did you measure up to these images? What kind of courage was required to control your insecurities enough to reach out to others and allow them to know you?

We are routinely told that adolescence and young adulthood are supposed to be the happiest years of our lives. In fact, this time is fraught with failed experiments in human relationships. Because our parents and schools give us little useful information about how to live in the world, we are engaged in an exercise of trial-and-error learning. Some of the errors, notably social rejection, are extremely painful, and most of us develop a persona that allows us to minimize this pain. Those who have the accidental gifts of athletic ability or conventional beauty tend to do best at this stage of life. The rest of us try to control our anxieties and develop alternative identities by finding

Nothing prepares us for the terrible risk of intimacy.

others who share our interests and our developing philosophy of what constitutes worldly success. This urge to be around like-minded peers is the basis for the (universally mispronounced) cliques that characterize life in high school.

I recently went back to my (all-male) fifty-fifth high school reunion and was astonished at the different memories we all had of that time together. Gone with the years was the sense of losing the social competition that is *my* most vivid memory of that period. The water that had flowed under each of our bridges had washed away the feelings of not being good enough or attractive enough or smart enough to succeed in the impenetrably complicated game of life. Each of us seems to have made his separate peace with his journey, now drawing to a close, and with each other. The old pictures we passed around were of people impossibly young, with different values and no accomplishment. We felt a bond of familiarity that flowed from those years spent together, but I think we all would have liked a moment of time travel to reassure those young faces that they would find a way to resolve their insecurities and would find someone to love them, and that life would present other things more important to worry about than adolescent anxieties.

Of the many things we didn't know when we were

eighteen, the most important was how to recognize the person who would consent to share our fates. The girls we were in contact with appeared to inhabit an alternate universe and to have limited interest in us. That they had veto power over relationships in which we were expected to take the initiative seemed especially unfair. That they had their own confusion and insecurity about not being chosen was not apparent. From our point of view, they were unreasonably withholding their approval. This perception generated some attitudes that affected many of us for a long time, notably anger at the evident unfairness and power disparity. The entire scene was a laboratory for anxiety, though we never confessed this to each other.

In this environment, not surprisingly, we had trouble learning what the military calls the "rules of engagement." The culture that surrounded us, which we breathed like air, suggested certain roles and behaviors that were inimical to what we were looking for, closeness and respect, though we were also unaware at the time that this is what we needed. Instead, the lessons we were taught had more to do with dominance, manipulation, and an implied contract for services that presumed specific gender-based roles that, if well played, would lead to satisfying and enduring relationships. Little did we know what awaited us when these roles became unsatisfying to women, who eventually demanded their share of the American pie that they had heretofore simply been expected to bake. Not surprisingly, the divorce rate began its climb to 50 percent of marriages, where it remains. We were so surprised!

These changes didn't happen all at once, and not everyone was affected in the same way. We can still find marriages, especially between religious people, operating under nineteenth- and early twentieth-century contracts. But in general, young people are navigating new territory when it comes to relationships. They do, however, still struggle with the question of what constitutes a successful choice of partner, whom to avoid and whom to cherish, which character traits are dangerous and which wear well over time. Even in our old age, many of us still appear not to have grasped a fundamental truth: In our search for happiness, we are entitled to receive only that which we are prepared to give.

So over the years, we have come to a different definition of what constitutes courage in our search for intimacy. Our primary fears in this venture are humiliation and rejection, which is why relationships between the sexes are so fraught with competition and why so many marriages involve struggles for control. Some think that infidelity, traditionally the province of men (though women seem to be catching up), is simply a search for sexual variety. In my experience, however, going outside the marriage reflects deep-seated anger at one's partner and is a tactic in the power struggles that characterize so many relationships, especially those in which gender roles are blurred and the partners are expected to be on equal footing. The betrayal that infidelity represents is a profoundly hostile act that permanently alters relationships, whether or not reconciliation and forgiveness allow them to continue.

If the choice is to reconstitute the marriage, both people live with the knowledge that one of them intentionally hurt the other in the most profound way. More than a violation of a promise ("forsaking all others"), infidelity is an unmistakable indicator of selfishness, and anger on the part of someone in whom we have reposed our best hopes. A couple may have compelling reasons to stay together—children, finances, a belief that we are all imperfect and prone to "mistakes"—but a mask has slipped and what has been revealed cannot be made new.

Confronted by such risks, we still persist in our search for love. If we misjudge our first attempts at intimacy, we try again. The alternative is loneliness, which for most of us is intolerable for long. Sometimes we learn from our mistakes, more often not; the rate of failure in second and third marriages is greater than that of our first attempts. We are distracted by superficial qualities and imagine that we are good judges of character when we are clearly not. This deficit in discrimination, this inability to discern who is loyal and kind and dependable over time, costs us dearly, and we may grow cynical and self-protective. And our searches go on as if love were a scarce and nonrenewable resource that we must bargain for in the most self-protective way. Marriage as an institution is not failing us; we are failing it.

Life is not a rehearsal.

*The worst sorrows in life are not in its
losses and misfortune but in its fears.*

—A. C. Benson

Fear can be photographed as a nearly universal expression on people's faces; courage is expressed in actions that are, in general, impossible to capture in a single image. Many of those who display it, sometimes over a period of years, did not realize that they had such a capacity within them. Often they do not think of themselves as especially brave: "I was doing my job," "It was my responsibility," "I did it without thinking." But courage is always an act of love that reflects a belief in something larger than ourselves. Some people are willing to die for an idea, such as freedom or truth. Others are prepared to sacrifice themselves for those they love, and still others appear to have a more inclusive sense of brotherhood that impels them to take great risks for strangers. Some are drawn to dangerous occupations as a way of testing themselves to see whether they are brave.

Our ceaseless search for heroes often leads us up the blind alley of notoriety, as with movie stars and athletes, or becomes a synonym for competence, as in the physician whose skill saves lives. There is also the formulaic story of a heretofore unknown person whose job requires taking risks that most of us do not face. This heroic status can quickly be generalized to all who put on a uniform in public service ("New York's bravest"). If a part of one's job description is to enter burning buildings, does one become a hero if the building collapses? How heroic is the soldier whose vehicle is blown up as he drives down the road? Presumably, in volunteering for the military, for reasons patriotic or otherwise, he assumed that risk. Is a parent who throws herself on her child to save him from a tornado exhibiting heroism or simply the same reflex observable in nearly all animals to protect their young?

Perhaps we need to expand our timeline in our search for people to admire. We daily observe those who have given a significant part of their lives to the service of others, those who have given up their chance at the conventional definition of success to work among the poor or the handicapped. In such cases, we come up against the difference between generosity and bravery. Anyone who devotes his life to helping others is undeniably generous. Most people who make this choice, however, do not assume the risk that courage requires. Parents who decide to raise a handicapped child as an alternative to institutionalization are deserving of admiration. They are giving up a significant part of the conventional vision of what it is to be a parent on behalf of the small human being who needs their care but will never be the person they dreamed of raising. All the virtues on display in such a situation—steadfastness, loyalty, commitment—make them infinitely more deserving of respect than most of the people we are taught to admire or elevate to the status of hero. Yet to call them courageous is stretching the definition of the word. We are accustomed to describing as courageous those who regain their health after serious illness or injury. But did they have a choice?

People who decide to parent double-digit numbers of children, born to them or adopted, are commonly celebrated. Perhaps I have seen too many of these situations that have not worked well for these kids for me to join in the applause. While love may be infinite, time is not. At some point, we cannot give enough of ourselves to each child in a huge family, occasionally with disastrous results. I am especially dubious about cultures and religions that demand "full quivers" of children so that their faith or philosophy can be carried by their children as "arrows" into the future. This instrumental view of parenthood smacks of a certainty of righteousness that meets the needs of parents at the expense of the independent people our children will become.

If courage is a virtue worth cultivating, how do we do so in a world in which a constant push exists to reduce risk? We train our children to be safe, to be wary of strangers, to fasten their seatbelts, to look both ways before crossing the street. We cannot bear the thought of losing them to carelessness. We hover over them as if we can protect them from all harm. The message we are sending to them with our concern is that unnecessary risk is to be avoided. Where are the trials, the rites of passage that characterize primitive societies, in which risk is accepted as inevitable? Instead of requiring that they kill a lion, we put our kids through bar mitzvahs, test their driving ability, or make it legal for them to drink alcohol. Contact sports remain the only real tests of physical determination and effort for those who care about such things. People who devote themselves to academic excellence are usually rewarded, but this is an essentially self-centered pursuit of little immediate benefit to others.

The things that preoccupy our young people these days are nearly all the pursuits of the self-involved. The social media that occupy so much of their time are designed for those who imagine that the minutiae of their lives are of interest to others. It is hard to read many tweets or look at many Facebook pages without a sense that informing others about our most insignificant thoughts and activities betrays only how superficial and trivial they are. We appear to have accepted narcissism as a healthy character trait and are training an entire generation to adopt it. When a prominent figure in the society is found to be using his Twitter account to send explicit pictures of himself, we are (gleefully) shocked. He has gone too far in sharing his admiration for himself. The rest of us are just keeping our "friends" informed of everything we are thinking and doing. We are rendering ourselves stupid by filling our brains with trivia to the exclusion of whatever more important information or knowledge might reside there if we were given to reflection.

A virtuous society is inhabited by virtuous people. To acquire the traits that allow us to act generously toward each other, we must have people to admire who display them, who can serve as examples to the rest of us. Where are we to find such people? Who are most visible, celebrated by the media, followed by photographers, and handed microphones so that they might entertain us? We who do not qualify for such attention seek it out. We line up to participate in reality shows, we jostle others to be on television, however briefly. Look at those people in crowd scenes holding up signs, waving and screaming maniacally when a camera is pointed at them. Who are they waving at? For that moment, they exist in a way not usually available to them as anonymous members of the audience. Not long ago, at a performance in Las Vegas, Cher made a grand entrance in a gilded cage over the heads of the crowd. When she arrived onstage she said, "You know, if I fell out of that thing, tomorrow's headline would read, 'Cher killed in freak accident.' Underneath, it would say, 'Five faceless fans also die when she falls on them.'" She concluded with the moral of the story, "I love being famous."

Most of us come to accept the reality that we are spectators to a show in which we will never be expected to perform. This perception of ourselves is why if something happens in front of us that invites action or intervention, our first impulse is to watch rather than to act, particularly if we perceive a risk. From our largest spectacles to the private struggles of the people around us, we have been trained to be passive observers. Our television screens have been so long filled with pain, injustice, and inhumanity that most of us have lost our capacity for outrage and action, especially if the faces we see are a different color or from a distant place. Without our being aware of it, our souls have withered and we turn away or imagine that what we are seeing could not happen to us or those we love. We are worse than cowards, who at least know what they should do; we have become numbed and helpless in the face of human suffering. We change the channel to something more entertaining.

16

Courage is like love;
it must have hope to nourish it.

People react to fear, not love—they don't teach that
in Sunday School, but it's true.

—Richard Nixon

Hopelessness is the ultimate failure of imagination. The most prosaic form of courage is a willingness to get out of bed each morning and continue our lives. In the face of work that does not inspire us, relationships that have become stale and weighted with failed expectations, a world that little resembles the dreams of our youth, most of us choose to go on. *What gives us hope that things will change for the better?*

This is the essential question in psychotherapy (which is defined as conversation directed at change) and is expressed in a more succinct question with which I confront patients: "What's next?" We waste a lot of time thinking about the past, or that version of it that we choose to explain the present. We frequently talk about the importance of hope without specifying what we are hoping for. For hope to be genuine, it must be realistic; otherwise it is but a dream. Visualize the long lines that form at lottery outlets when the payoff reaches hundreds of millions of dollars. My state lottery has as its motto "You've got to play to win." A more realistic slogan would be, "You've got to play to lose." Obviously, hope impels people to stand in those lines, discussing how they will spend their winnings. The problem is that this hope is undone by odds that make it unrealistic and result in many spending money they cannot afford. The hope for miracles also provides fertile ground for those who would sell us cancer cures, effortless weight loss programs, real estate with no money down, "natural" remedies, untold wealth from Nigeria, or shortcuts to finding the perfect mate. Those who tell others how to live don't get rich advocating perseverance, loyalty, or years of education. Where's the fun in that?

We are in love with new ideas, the big score, the sudden transformation. We ignore the truth that I have written about elsewhere: *Only bad things happen quickly.* Why do most kids hate school? Why is the slow acquisition of knowledge boring? Why do we appear to have such short historical memories? Why does the stock market fluctuate so unpredictably, exactly like one's bankroll in a Las Vegas casino? All these things occur because we are distracted from the real purpose of our lives by a dream of effortless success, narrowly defined in our culture as the accumulation of worldly goods. The core concept of capitalism—that we can all prosper together—has given way to a kind of societal selfishness that is an invitation to class conflict based on envy and a sense of unfairness. An expression of and an outlet for the longing to be rich is the false idea that we too, with a little luck, can have it all.

What is lost in such fragile hopes is the concept of pride in our work, the satisfaction that comes with doing our jobs well in the knowledge that we can construct a comfortable, if not extravagant, life as a result of our labors. Stalked by recession, unemployment, home foreclosures, stagnating income, jobs moving overseas, and endless warfare, we can easily grow angry and cynical. When this anger is redirected at minorities—immigrants, gay people, government workers—we are in danger of becoming fragmented along the lines of race and class, prisoners of our fear that there is not enough to go around and that we must each act in our own economic interest. This formula relinquishes the central idea of the society: interdependence, that we are all in this together and will succeed or fail based on our ability to cooperate with and care about others.

If everything worthwhile in this life—education, loving relationships, occupational skill, the development of civic virtue—requires sustained effort, who will teach us to let go of the idea of instant gratification? The degree to which we covet the latest electronic gadget bodes ill for this effort. Are the thoughts being shared on a $500 iPhone any more compelling than those we used to write down and put in a mailbox? Have you read anything significant on Twitter recently? How many Facebook friends do you have? How many of them could you count on for help at 3 A.M.?

To face the future with courage, we must believe that we have the power, the resolve, and the tolerance to contribute to a world that we and our children will want to live in. Americans have much of which to be proud and

Courage is like love; it must have hope to nourish it.

some things of which to be ashamed. To get where we want to go, we must have at least general agreement on where we have been. We need, in other words, to know our history. Our forbears created a system of democratic government that has been a beacon to all who would live in freedom, but they also tolerated slavery. We won the wars, hot and cold, against Fascism and Communism, but we also interned our fellow citizens based on their race. We think of ourselves as peace loving while spending more on our military than do all other nations combined. We elected a black president, but discrimination against others for inborn circumstances such as race, sexual orientation, and national origin persists. We may be "exceptional," but like all humans, we are fallible and given to the conceit of those who have easier lives than most.

As a psychiatrist, I sell hope in individual doses. I listen to people's stories, question their fundamental beliefs about themselves, and try to help them identify and change those parts of their lives that are keeping them from being happy or fulfilled. My view of how people in groups see themselves and each other is informed by my belief that much of what we think we know is untrue and most of our behavior is driven by desires and motives of which we are only dimly aware. I also believe that insight, generosity, and tolerance are not inborn traits but can be taught. We just have to identify those among us who are qualified to lead and teach us. They must be intelligent and devoted to the principles of kindness and hope. If, instead, we elevate those who are stupid or arrogant (or both), we will get the future we deserve.

17

Punishment and revenge
are the favored responses
of fearful people.

To hate and to fear is to be psychologically ill . . .
it is, in fact, the consuming illness of our time.
—Harry A. Overstreet

What is fear other than anticipation of the worst?
From the smallest threat we can conjure disaster.
Learning how to tolerate, even embrace, uncertainty,
with an anticipation of good outcomes leavened by the
reality of risk, underlies every conception of courage.
As with all things, the middle road between fear and

complacency is the only path upon which we can pursue happiness in the face of our mortality.

If it is true that in life we are more likely to get not what we deserve but what we expect, how can we adjust our expectations in the direction of optimism without becoming naïve? In our interactions with other people, we betray what we anticipate by the way we behave, our facial expression, the tone of our voice. How many times have we seen visibly irritated people at airline counters or hotel registration desks testing the patience of those trying to help them? Among the most revealing behaviors in our repertoire are the way we treat those who are providing us a service: waiters, retail clerks, cab drivers. These interactions are so important that I routinely ask about them when talking to those questioning whether to proceed with marriage to a particular person. Self-absorbed people tend to have unrealistic expectations about how the world will accommodate them and are inflexible and easily angered under stress. The expectation that the world will recognize their specialness and usher them to the head of the line often evokes resentment that results in poorer rather than better service.

In the area of health care, for example, I have witnessed enough medical mistakes to know that some people have more trouble than others getting good care.

Some such errors are randomly distributed and the fault of providers; others appear to be a commentary on the patience of the patient. For example, one woman I know was notoriously critical and demanding of the nursing staff. But she wondered why she had trouble getting her call button answered and was the victim of an above-average number of errors in her medication dosages. These events, of course, only reinforced her convictions about the general incompetence of her caregivers.

Our choice of attitude and its consequences is important in how we confront our fears. Survivors of natural disasters, shocked by the devastation around them, routinely talk about rebuilding. The pastor stands in the ruins of his church, faith intact. Because God's ways are beyond our comprehension, He gets all the credit and none of the blame, whatever happens. First among our fears, it seems, is the loneliness implicit in the idea that we might live in an indifferent universe.

Somewhere between the narcissistic belief that we individually are the center of creation and the conception that we are actors in a preordained play is a large area in which we operate under the constraints of time and chance but still have choices about how to live. Whether our lives are dominated by anxiety and selfishness or we choose to cope with our fears through generosity and tolerance determines the kind of world we create for ourselves and each other. This dichotomy of behavior is seldom discussed when we argue about decisions concerning standards of personal conduct or philosophies of government. But all our conceptions of how to live, individually and collectively, hinge on beliefs about our responsibilities toward each other and our respect for people's rights to live in ways different from our own.

We are in danger here of a self-fulfilling prophecy, in which some are permanently disadvantaged by a social system that favors the wealthy and neglects or punishes the less powerful. Such unfairness produces a resentment and cynicism that poison our attempts to live peacefully with one another. These battles may be fought on grounds of constitutionalism and the role of government in our lives, but the underlying issues of fairness, fear, and civic duty must be brought into the debate if we are to reach an understanding. Not since we fought a civil war over slavery, another disagreement over what it means to be human, have the stakes been as high.

Life shrinks or expands in proportion to one's courage.

The important thing is this: To be able at any moment
to sacrifice what we are for what we could become.
—Charles DeBois

The size and shape of the lives we lead depend on our ability to engage with others about ideas and emotions. No one is born with a heart full of feelings and a head full of thoughts, so we are in a more or less continuous state of learning. To open ourselves to other people and new experiences requires a special sort of humility that resists the forces of calcified prejudice.

I have found that much of what passes for conventional wisdom is untrue. An example of this deficit in thinking is contained in the aphorism "What does not kill us makes us stronger." These words, misguided and false, are frequently offered to those grieving a serious loss in their lives. Bereaved parents hear this maxim as a form of consolation and are left to contemplate how anyone can be strengthened by the death of their child. "Good relationships require hard work" is another truism that I think of as a probable commentary on the marriage of the person offering it. Clichés foster a kind of pseudo-knowledge that clutters our brains, impeding our ability to think about old problems in a new way.

Viewed unsparingly, most of our troubles, though they may seem unique to us, are old and have been confronted by many others before us. Knowing this, we face the truth that our only choice when we have been wounded is how to react. The process of grief, for example, is one of intense self-absorption. We are, after the loss of someone we love, like soldiers who have been pinned down in combat: afraid to move but knowing that, if we do not, our lives are over.

We have been trained to respond passively to misfortune. I think of this as the medical model of crisis management. When we become sick or are injured, we are taught to rest and let someone else minister to us. If we are *very* sick, we are placed in hospitals where we are put to bed in ridiculous gowns and are expected, like children, to follow orders from the people in charge. Little emphasis is given to participating in our own care or doing anything ourselves that might foster healing.

In many other areas of our lives, we put ourselves in the hands of "experts" who presume to advise us on how to live. This attitude is a major problem in psychotherapy. Many patients come to me expecting sage advice (and prescriptions for medication) that will alter their emotional lives for the better. Among my harder tasks is to convince them that the answers must come from within them and that it is my job to ask the questions that will enable them to find solutions that fit their lives. I can serve as a source of accountability for changing their behaviors in the desired direction. I can also correct some misconceptions about their predicaments and tell them what I have learned over the years about emotional healing, especially the importance of hope. Many people are intolerant of such an approach, which expects them to take responsibility for themselves, and leave disappointed that I cannot offer them the rapid and definitive solutions they desire.

Whenever I invoke courage in undertaking the process of change, I know that I am flying in the face of societal expectations. Few of our institutions, apart from the military and sports, ever mention the importance of being brave in the face of adversity. It seems to me ironic that one of the newer diagnoses to sweep across the psychiatric landscape is adult attention deficit disorder, that form of distractibility that has as its treatment the regular use of stimulant drugs, including methamphetamine. I remember the seriousness with which psychiatry not so long ago considered multiple personality disorder, recovered memory syndrome, and various forms of "addiction," including shopping and viewing pornography.

We often attach a diagnostic label to certain behaviors such as drinking as a means of relieving stigma and encouraging participation in a 12-step program. Unfortunately, the implication that people suffer from an illness also relieves them from some of the individual responsibility for change and relapse. If they are sick, how can we hold them accountable? Alcoholics Anonymous, with its emphasis on abstinence and with a low tolerance for excuses, has been the most successful form of treatment for those who drink to excess. Extending this model to gambling and promiscuous sex may work for some, but the idea that every bad habit deserves a diagnosis ignores the reality that most human behavior, good and bad, is habitual and that both vice and virtue are commentaries on how we see ourselves in relation to others.

The psychopaths in our midst, for example, unencumbered by conscience, are only doing what they perceive to be in their self-interest. They are not "sick" nor do they want to change. The courtroom, not the mental health clinic, is the appropriate place to deal with them. Those who do want to change habitual behaviors must invoke their capacity for courage and determination. If they can find a group that encourages them to do so, they are fortunate. But first they need to stop watching talk shows that encourage them to feel like victims of circumstance. The traumas of our youth, including our imperfect parents, no doubt played a role in our adult distress but are an insufficient excuse for our current refusal to change unwanted behaviors.

Recognizing that we have the freedom to choose is a hallmark of mental health. In the grip of anxiety or depression, we have fewer choices because our lives are circumscribed by our avoidance behaviors. Years ago, I had a patient who was terrified of birds. When outside, she was constantly on the alert for them; she would cross the street to avoid them. We looked at pictures of birds, and later, I brought a caged bird from a nearby pet shop into the sessions. Eventually I was able to release the bird in the room. At our last meeting, she came in a dress covered with images of birds. Her life had been expanded and made easier because she had the determination to rid herself of this irrational apprehension.

Most of our anxieties are, of course, more complicated and involve relationships with other people. And yet the willingness to confront what we fear remains the touchstone of successful treatment. The only word for this belief in our own capacity to heal is courage.

Cowardice is the incapacity to love anything but oneself.

The human race is a race of cowards, and I am not only marching in that procession but carrying a banner.

—Mark Twain

Of all the disadvantages of our congenital narcissism, the challenge of devoting our lives to people and ideas apart from ourselves remains paramount. What is required to encourage cooperative and unselfish behavior?

A well-known religious self-help book begins with these words: "It's not about you." Whatever "it" is (life, presumably), the objective appears to be to stop being so self-absorbed and turn our faces toward God. I've never liked this idea but not because it invokes the power of faith; countless examples of good works have been performed in the name of religion. My objection to using religious belief as the primary basis for morality is that such a conviction is another way of attributing our difficulties to people and forces outside ourselves and over which we have little control. To say that God is the source of all virtue is similar to attributing our individual limitations to our past experience. Both beliefs diminish our own responsibility for behaving well in the present and constructing a future of which we can be proud, whether or not it includes salvation for our immortal souls.

Just as one can be brave in many ways, cowardice takes different forms. We all have situations and people who intimidate us physically. By the time we finish elementary school, most of us have some experience of bullying. If we have not been bullied ourselves, we have seen others picked on because of some physical or emotional departure from the group norm. Our reaction to this first hint of life's unfairness is usually to endure or try to ignore it, particularly if it is happening to someone else. And so is set in motion the familiar "bystander phenomenon," in which we attempt to avoid things that do not directly affect us. Such an attitude is good preparation for the kind of cowardice that will enable us to walk or drive by our fellow human beings in distress on city streets or to avert our eyes from the many other forms of injustice that the world contains. How many people can we be expected to care about, after all?

Self-centeredness, usually thought of in individual terms, can also apply to those whom we see as belonging to the same tribe. If you draw a diagram showing personal attachments, you will discover who really matters to you. Our core loyalties are to our family, friends, and members of our immediate community, however we define community. Those we care about tend to be people like us, in race, education, and social class. These allegiances can be further extended to include regional or national attachments but seldom extend much beyond that. Circumscribed loyalty is why it is easier to ignore (or even kill) those who are discernibly different from us in language, ethnicity, or religion. This fact is the basis for the dehumanization of the enemy that accompanies every war. By virtue of being different, their lives are somehow less valuable.

And so our sense of responsibility for or caring about others is a test of inclusiveness. The degree of risk we are willing to take on behalf of other human beings is a test of our attachment to them, which is why unit cohesiveness is so important to the military. If the mutual welfare of those in a unit becomes a dominant value, people will routinely take life-threatening risks on each other's behalf. "Band of brothers" is an apt description of an infantry unit in combat. People are much more likely to hazard their lives for a person than an idea. Personal survival and caring for each other's welfare are the primary reasons for fighting bravely. In fact, the willingness to risk one's life on behalf of another is the operational definition of love.

Cowardice may be thought of as surrender to fear. This emotion represents the "flight" alternative in the well-known fight-or-flight phenomenon that oversimplifies the human response to danger. In any threatening situation, risk assessment is critical to survival. If we are confronted by overwhelming force, we are behaving adaptively to try to escape rather than fight and die. In the modern world, we seldom face occasions in which our lives are threatened. Instead, we are more likely to encounter our fellow human beings in distress and simply have to decide whether and how much we are prepared to help them.

"Cowardice" is usually not the word applied to a willingness to tolerate injustice, perhaps because each of us is

Cowardice is the incapacity to love anything but oneself.

aware of situations in which we ought to have acted in someone's defense yet chose not to. And we know that how we behave in such instances is a measure of our sense of common humanity. Whatever the source for our morality—religious, philosophical, or situational—we all know that the protection of the weak from exploitation by the strong is a fundamental obligation of any civilized person. My local library is participating in a program designed to improve our interactions with each other. At the various library branches, one can pick up bumper stickers that read, "Choose civility." (After being cut off by a few vehicles bearing this message, I have been tempted to get a bumper sticker that reads, "Forget civility; learn how to drive.") The appeal to politeness on the road is laudable, but I think that more than courtesy is required of us if we are to sustain our commitments to each other. I would opt for a bumper sticker that said simply "Courage," except that I doubt most people would understand such a cryptic message any more than they did when Dan Rather ended his CBS newscast years ago with this attempt at encouragement.

20

Honesty is a prerequisite for courage.

When I am honest, I am automatically humble.

—Hugh Prather

My first exposure to large-scale lying came when I was a platoon leader with the 82nd Airborne Division in 1961. President Kennedy was scheduled to pay a visit to Ft. Bragg, North Carolina, to inspect our readiness to intervene anywhere in the world. The division was laid out on the airfield, with each battle group dressed for combat in a different environment. One battle group wore uniforms for jungle fighting, another was in brown for desert warfare. My battle group was clothed all in white and posing with skis to demonstrate our readiness to fight on some frozen landscape in northern Europe or Asia. It was darkly humorous that many of my men had never seen snow, much less trained to fight in it. Like most Army units at the time, the 82nd was well below full strength, so among our ranks that day were soldiers from various support units at Bragg—cooks, truck drivers, clerks—most of whom were not even parachute qualified.

We must have made an impressive picture as Air Force One slowly circled the airfield. I wondered if it was a good idea for the president to be under the impression that he was looking at a full-strength, combat-ready airborne division, available on short notice to fight wherever the country needed them.

Any decision to overcome fear must be accompanied by a realistic assessment of resources, risk, and a rational decision about whether the outcome is worth the hazard. Sometimes, as in battle, there is little time to think. The choice to throw oneself on a grenade to save people nearby may be a reflex, but one born of a commitment previously undertaken.

Most acts that we think of as courageous are the product of some reflection. The passengers on United Flight 93 on September 11 had time to contemplate their predicament. They had news of other airliners being flown into buildings and so came to understand their certain fate if they did nothing. Within minutes they were able to make the decision to fight to gain control of the cockpit and organize themselves to confront the hijackers. Their telephone conversations with people on the ground reveal both fear and a determination to try to save themselves.

Few of us are likely to be confronted with such life-threatening decisions. The fears we face are, in general, long term and involve questions related to how to find meaningful work, to take care of each other, to figure out whom to love, to meet our obligations to those who depend on us, to cope with the depredations of age, and, finally, to face our mortality.

Few of us are taught systematically about the importance of these tasks, much less how to accomplish them. Instead, the culture is oriented toward distraction and entertainment and preoccupied with safety. Honesty as a value is honored more in the breach than in the observance. Stories of people returning found money are much less numerous than those that illustrate the many ways we take advantage of one other.

The process of being elected to office, especially high office, is driven by relentless ambition and routinely involves fraud and dissembling. An honest politician has become an oxymoron. Hypocrisy, the worst form of dishonesty, is at once an object of our contempt and accepted as an occupational hazard among those who would deceive us for power or profit. The widespread cynicism that this reality produces undermines the trust essential to any political system that depends on the consent of the governed.

Of all the phenomena that have come to characterize the American political process, the rise of disrespect, even hatred, on the part of those who disagree on matters of religion or politics is perhaps the most ominous development. Some characterize this display as a decline in civility, but it is more than that. The attribution of ill will or a lack of patriotism to one's opponents bespeaks a loss of faith in our ability to listen to, learn from, and compromise with each other. Ignorance, anger, and fear are coexisting traits that have come to distort the public discourse, leading to all manner of conspiracy theories and delusional beliefs. Science itself is discounted in arguments over topics such as evolution and climate change. When we abandon the scientific method as a way of understanding the world, we take leave of reason, and any assertion—no matter how crazy—can become a fixed belief.

Nature itself is intolerant of stupidity. If one is disoriented in the wilderness or lost at sea, survival depends on an ability to navigate and find food. We may be insulated from such harsh reality by the conveniences of modern life and the proximity of the local supermarket, but we are still in danger of losing our way individually and as a society if we lose the capacity to listen to each other and act in a way that benefits all.

We cannot allow ourselves to be lied to or, worse, to engage in a process of self-deception. In psychotherapy, I am continually confronted with this problem. I point out to people that many things we believe about overselves turn out to be untrue. As examples, I cite the "three great lies" that nearly all of us tell ourselves: I'm a good driver; I have a good sense of humor; I'm a good judge of character. That these are characteristics that we all share is evidently not true, but each of us clings to the belief that we are the exception.

We need each other if we are to construct a courageous society. As long as we are not alone, there is nothing that we cannot face. And we are never out of options. In the desperation of the concentration camps of World War II, the psychiatrist Viktor Frankl concluded that "the last human freedom is the ability to choose the attitude with which we meet our fate."

Courage begins with understanding. If we learned to be more honest with ourselves about our strengths and our failings, perhaps we would be in a position to demand more from those we choose to lead us. Here is the truth: *We are all fallible and none of us is selfless* (some of us have even made a virtue of selfishness). No one has all the answers, and we all deserve tolerance for our shortcomings. But we need to be as truthful with ourselves as we can be so that we can demand honesty and forbearance from those we select to make decisions about the common good.

Fear springs from ignorance.

It is when power is wedded to chronic fear
that it becomes formidable.

—Eric Hoffer

We are afraid of what we do not understand. If life is a process of discovery, we are in a constant search for guidance. Our imperfect maps of how the world works have many blank areas, and like the cartographers of old, we fill these spaces with dragons. We begin to control our fears in our battles against ignorance.

The first step in understanding fear is to recognize those similarities of emotion and purpose that we share with others. All human connections are temporary and subject to change. Although people nearly always see themselves as good judges of character, the success of Ponzi schemes, the response to emails promising great wealth for little effort, and our divorce rate all demonstrate that we are fallible in our attempts to judge the character and intentions of others. We repose our hopes in those we imagine we can trust, only to be surprised when they do not deliver what they promised. With equal frequency, we are disappointed in ourselves when we fail to meet our own expectations of accomplishment and fidelity.

Fear and cynicism lie at the heart of our difficulty establishing trust. Because long-term relationships fail at such a painful and spectacular rate, our efforts to protect ourselves from disappointment are natural. However, attempts to avoid heartbreak undermine our ability to commit ourselves fully, which is our only hope of getting what we truly want.

In a larger sense we are betrayed by our tendency to place outside ourselves the responsibility for the disparity between what we have and what we wish for. We appear to have a fundamental desire to blame others for what happens to us. We are entertained by a culture of victimization. Our upbringings are mined to discover shortcomings in our parents that would explain our unhappiness. We form organizations aimed at exploring the consequences of parental alcoholism, abuse, and neglect. We gather with others who have had similar experiences and whose lives have been warped by their pasts. As vehicles for understanding what has happened to us, these efforts have merit; as a way of displacing responsibility for our present and future, they are less useful. I have written elsewhere about invoking a "statute of limitations" on our childhood traumas. Again, the attachment to a sense of victimization is a form of fear about what we need to do to overcome our pasts.

Many fears can dominate our lives: fear of intimacy, failure, responsibility, the rapid passage of time, and death. Why is there so little discussion of these natural human apprehensions and how to mobilize the courage to live optimistic, authentic lives in the face of them? Wouldn't you imagine that such subjects ought to occupy a significant portion of every high school curriculum? What does it say about us that we seldom talk about such things with our children? Instead, their heads (and ours) are filled with the most superficial images of worldly success.

It is ironic that we lavish so much worry on our children's development and safety while ignoring the real risks to their future happiness. We transmit to them in ways large and small our sense that the world is dangerous and unpredictable. We worry that they will smoke, drink, or engage in dangerous sex. We have an exaggerated sense of our power to shape their lives. We devour conflicting advice from "experts" about how to raise exceptional (or at least above average) children. We put bumper stickers on our cars attesting to their successes. And yet we give little attention to what we are teaching them by our example. How often do our children see us reading a book, acting in a generous way toward a stranger, thoughtfully discussing an idea, expressing affection to a spouse, demonstrating gratitude for a kindness? Some adults, not you of course, go days without doing any of these things. Do we imagine that values are taught through lectures and criticism? Why do young people pay more attention to each other and to their cultural heroes than they do their parents? The families I see in therapy are usually embroiled in conflict with children who openly express disrespect for their parents. But what of the larger number of families in which parents are simply seen by their kids as having little that is relevant to teach them? Indifference is in some ways worse than hostility.

The less information we have about something (or someone), the more threatened we are likely to feel about it (or them). With the increasing polarization of cable news, most of us now learn about the world by listening to people with whom we agree politically and philosophically. Newspapers, more reliable sources of objective information, are dying, and the Internet is a Wild West mélange of fact, fable, and opinion that is now the primary source of news, especially for the young. The commentators with the greatest popularity are unabashed partisans who thrive in an atmosphere of apocalyptic controversy. Reason is replaced by emotion, and those with opposing views are routinely demonized as unpatriotic, subversive, or uninformed.

This atmosphere of confrontation and fear mongering gives rise to political figures who stake out extreme positions and pander to the 25 percent of the population receptive to conspiracy theories that threaten their conception of how the country should be governed. When sufficiently aroused, this portion of the electorate is large enough and well-enough funded that they can exercise a disproportionate influence on the electoral process. They tend to be religious, which adds to their fervor, and preoccupied with any perceived threat to their narrow definitions of virtue. They are nostalgic for a misremembered past when there was less crime and more respect for authority, when the country was led by white men, when we had never lost a war (except, of course, for the Civil War), and when women and minorities knew their places, everyone believed in God, extended families lived together, few people got divorced, children were more tractable, music more comprehensible and less loud, and hardly anyone knew someone who was gay. The fact that white people will be in the minority in the United States by 2050 is an extremely uncomfortable reality for a significant portion of the population.

This group tends to have rigid ideas about child rearing and a fondness for punishment as an instrument of social control. This philosophy, based on fear, can extend from a belief in corporal punishment for children to an enthusiasm for the death penalty unique in the Western world. The need to own handguns and assault rifles is a reflection of both fear that others may take what is yours by force and a belief that an armed populace is the ultimate defense against governmental tyranny. Women must be punished for irresponsible sex by being forced to bear unwanted children; this is characterized as a "right to life" and is based entirely on a religious definition of when life begins that must be enforced by the government.

What is absent in this quarter of our fellow citizens is the idea that others with different beliefs deserve toleration. This coercive aspect of fundamentalist conviction causes the rest of us to feel that we are getting a whiff of theocracy at work. Those who would blur the lines between church and state, who are eager to inject prayer into the public space, who see the Ten Commandments as the basis of our legal system, and who perceive the world as a twilight struggle between the forces of good and evil are not likely to welcome the multicultural society that we are moving toward. In this sense, they are similar to the fanatics in the Muslim world, whose ideology is likewise based on ancient and infallible texts and is at war with modernity.

We struggle to make peace with the past, at least that part of it we can agree on, but our real task is to come to terms with a future that we may never see but which we are in the process of shaping. That unimaginable world, inhabited by our grandchildren and their grandchildren, must (if we are able to reach it at all) be a place where people are free to pursue their lives as they see fit, as long as they do not infringe on the rights of others to live according to their lights. The fears we must cope with as human beings should not be made worse by worries that those with different beliefs will force us to be like them.

22

It is pointless to fear the past.

A last letter to my birthmother:

Dear Ruth,

In our thirty years of knowing each other, two moments stand out: when first we met and when I saw you for the last time. At the age of thirty-five, I had just found out I was adopted. My parents, in their fear and insecurity, had omitted that detail during my upbringing. I think they felt guilty about buying me from the infamous Tennessee Children's Home so long ago. (Some people ponder their worth; I know mine exactly: $500.) They had a legal decree saying that I was theirs, but still, they must have wondered about the woman whose child they were raising.

Well, you know the story. I found out about my adoption, searched you out, and called. Here I was, an upstate New Yorker, talking to a stranger with a molasses Mississippi voice, imagining that I would have to convince her that I was who I said I was. I'll never forget your response: "What took you so long?" And so, you opened your door and your heart to me and I was looking at the first person, apart from my children, to whom I had a blood relationship. I was so glad that I hadn't let that lawyer in Memphis talk me into letting him find you. Whatever was going to happen was between us.

You were welcoming but afraid, glad to see that things had turned out well for me, but sure that I shared your own conviction that you "didn't live up to the moment" of my birth. I tried to reassure you that I understood what it must have been like to be a single schoolteacher in a small southern town, pregnant by a man you could not have. It must have been hard to spend those months in Memphis before I was born, far from home and under the control of people who wanted to sell your baby. And signing that piece of paper that let me go cost you so many years of regret, especially since you had already named me. But it was 1938 and you were alone. What else could you do? You carried your secret, and my adoptive parents carried theirs.

It is pointless to fear the past.

So I found you and told you of my life, including my four children, the youngest of whom, Michael, is adopted. You had remained single and told me that amazing story of changing the grade you taught each year in elementary school to correspond to the one you knew I must be in somewhere. Now I had returned, and you didn't know where I fit in your life or whether there was a place for you in mine. You had given birth to me, but could never be my mother. So you became a grandmother to my children, visiting, remembering birthdays. I have a picture of you and Michael and I marvel at the connections that life makes and what constitutes a family.

I don't think we ever got past the sadness of that long ago relinquishment. I thought I understood, but truthfully, looking at my own children, I could not imagine it. I don't think you ever forgave yourself, and our every contact was burdened by the thirty-five missing years. Yet we were friends. I took comfort in my biological connections; you were reassured that the son cast adrift had been loved and had found his way.

After the Alzheimer's began to steal you from me five years ago, it gave me a chance to say good-bye before your earthly connections faded entirely into forgetfulness. You did not speak my name on that last visit, perhaps because it is

different than the name you gave me. You were in a place
for the old in the town where you grew up—and I was
conceived—close to your roots, far from mine. Your
thoughts were veiled by a curtain of half-memories. I
wanted to ask if you ever thought about what we might
have been to each other. But I could not fill the past with
what it did not contain. Parted at birth, reunited as
strangers, "the years gone by with the blowing leaf" hung
between us still. I embraced you one last time and said
what I should have before: "Thank you for my life."

Love,

Gordon (born David)

Angus

I have only one picture of my father. It was taken at his
work when he was in his mid-forties. He stares solemnly and
without surprise at the camera, looking much the determined
businessman.

In the background are file cabinets, and in one corner of the
picture is the hand of another person holding a piece of paper
that awaits my father's attention. He is wearing a white shirt
and a paisley tie with an odd design spilling across it that I
cannot identify. I examine the photo with a magnifying glass,
like a detective or an archeologist trying to decipher its
meaning. I strain to see my face in his. It is all I have of him,

this snapshot. I have never heard his voice, never felt his touch.

He stares at me across the years, this man who gave me life and nothing more. I have questions for him, but he died before I could find him, before I was even aware he existed. My birth was the outcome of his hurried coupling with my mother on an October night in Vicksburg, Mississippi. It was a pathetically unsuccessful attempt by a lonely schoolteacher to bind this man to her. For him, I suppose she was a target of opportunity, and the resulting pregnancy, though no doubt embarrassing, was ultimately not his problem. He offered to finance an abortion, but something, perhaps having to go to New Orleans to get it, perhaps her religious family, perhaps even the hope that my father might change his mind and make an honest woman of her, gave her pause, and I was born.

She kept me only a week; he never saw me at all. I was left in the company of strangers who, fortunately, chose to love me as their own, only to have their hearts broken thirteen months later when the agency sold me to a couple who could pay. Many years afterward, I came looking for these shadowy people from my past. I found them all—except for my father, who had died, leaving behind this picture.

His name was Angus Hearn, so the Scottish ancestry provided by my adoptive parents was right after all. I wonder now what kind of life I would have lived in the delta country of

Mississippi. The people I found there, my birthmother and her family, speak with a euphonious lilt foreign to my Yankee ear ("Well, ah surely am glad t'see yew.") They are tolerant and kind, free of the small-town bigotry that was my own prejudiced expectation.

My mother had no other children, never married. My father, though, according to his obituary, did marry and had one daughter. This was exciting news; after a lifetime as an only child, I had a half-sister. I found out where she was and wrote her a letter introducing myself. She called immediately, excited also. It turned out, though, that Angus and his wife had adopted her, and she was contemplating a search for her origins.

Angus kept his secret even as Ruth kept hers and my adoptive parents kept theirs. All motives were at once benign and fearful: to protect themselves and those they loved or would love from the truth of my existence. But beneath these secrets lay other wishes less noble, more selfish: my birthparents that they had ignited a life and then abandoned it; my adoptive parents that they could not conceive and so chose to raise the child of strangers. The lie was preserved in a kind of bargain struck between two sets of parents who would never meet. And it was left to me to discover that I, simply by being born, was the source of the shame that all secrecy implies.

23

There are wounds that doctors cannot reach, that gratitude cannot heal.

*Memory and devotion. With them our hearts, though broken,
will be full and we will stay in the fight to the very last.*
—Mark Helprin, *A Soldier of the Great War*

Every year when Memorial Day rolls around, I listen to the predictable statements of appreciation for the sacrifices of those who have died in our nation's wars. They relinquished their futures at our behest, and we are obligated to be grateful.

When I was in Vietnam (1968–69), the first thing I noticed was that the actual fighting was done by the less than

20 percent of soldiers ("grunts") unfortunate enough to be assigned to the infantry or Marine rifle companies. There was, as I recall, little talk of freedom or democracy among them. The other 80 percent of our troops (REMFs) were busied driving trucks, maintaining PX facilities, sitting around some headquarters, or working as lifeguards at the Long Binh swimming pool. Now they are all Vietnam veterans whom we are expected to honor.

Another important discovery I made at war was that, in a combat unit, what separates the dead from the survivors is not courage but luck. The person who took the AK-47 round, stepped on the mine, bled to death before the medevac arrived was random. So when I look for a familiar name on the Vietnam Memorial in Washington, I do so with an appreciation for the power of chance. When I stand back far enough that I can see the entire black granite wall with its fifty-eight thousand names, the following questions cross my mind: What the hell was that for? What is here for the families of these men, the parents with fading memories, the grown children with no memories at all? Is my freedom more secure because of these sacrifices to the god of unintended consequences? How big a wall would it take to list the two million Vietnamese, north and south, killed while we were there?

There are wounds that doctors cannot reach, that gratitude cannot heal.

What we owe our veterans, living and dead, is the truth. For their losses (and our own) cannot be redeemed with sanctification or hyperbolic remembrance. It is easy to wax sentimental each Memorial Day about our unforgotten heroes. But if all we do is put on American Legion hats and lay wreaths and enshrine the memories of our unlucky countrymen, we miss the opportunity to learn something from their fates. Something about what happens when patriotism is equated to support for the latest military adventure—and who pays the price.

Since Vietnam, we have had Grenada, Panama, Dominican Republic, Beirut, Somalia, the 100-hour walkover in the Persian Gulf, the twenty-first-century adventures in Iraq and Afghanistan. Do the families of the men (and now women) lost in these places find themselves grateful and at peace with their sacrifices? I wish it were so, but I doubt it.

Sentimentality is a popular form of untruth. One example is the creation of heroes. Who better to nominate than those who have died defending the nation and its values? To bring out the flags and remember them once or twice a year seems little enough to ask of ourselves in the face of what they have lost. The problem with this ceremonial remembrance for me is that it seems self-indulgent. We cannot repay the families of our lost soldiers, families who must find consolation apart from the ceremonial remembrance of those who do not share their sacrifices. Rather than simply honoring the men and women we have lost, we are celebrating the notion that we live in a world in which we resolve conflicting ideas about how to live only by force. We tell ourselves that each military undertaking is required because some value—liberty, democracy—is threatened and must be defended. The instruments of such defense are the sons and daughters who are willing to hazard their lives if their country asks them to.

Next Memorial Day, before you join in romantic reverence for the dead with its implied willingness to add to that number, I ask you to think again about the cost, not of liberty, but of misjudgment. I would not wish on you my own memories of young men who, at the end, could only call for their mothers as their lives leaked away far from home.

24

Courage is required to bear the unbearable.

The life of every man is a diary in which he means to write
one story, and writes another; and his humblest hour is when
he compares the volume it is with what he vowed to make it.

—J. M. Barrie

On the wall of our bedroom hang two pictures. One is of my daughter Emily when she was eight. She is beautiful, smiling confidently into the camera, her arms crossed. The other is of her three-year-old brother, Lucas. He is on the cusp between a baby and a small boy. His blond hair is sparse, his mouth slightly open. He is

wearing a white sweater, and in his eyes is a look I con-
strue now as trust, a much-loved child who cannot imagine any harm befalling him.

The pictures were taken twenty-three years ago; the
colors have faded slightly. Emily graduated from law
school and works for a U.S. Senator. Lucas died in the
spring of 1992, at the age of six. Six months before his
death, he was diagnosed with acute myelocytic leukemia,
the result of the random mutation of a cell deep within
his otherwise perfect body. The odds of any child developing leukemia are roughly one in fifty thousand. The
struggle to save his life included chemotherapy and eventually a bone marrow transplant. I was the donor. My
marrow was not a perfect match, but it was close enough
that the doctors persuaded us to try the procedure since
his chances for survival without it were poor.

He developed something called graft versus host disease, which means that my transplanted cells attacked his
body and compromised his vital organs. He became
sicker and sicker until he bled uncontrollably, his stom-
ach was perforated, and he died. He was intubated and
unconscious near the end, but the moment when his
mother told him that he could stop struggling for life,
that we would all be okay and would see him in another
time and place is seared into my memory. I remember

the pictures of Hiroshima after the atomic bombing. There were shadows on the walls of people who had been vaporized by the explosion. I am afraid that if we went back to the Johns Hopkins Pediatric Intensive Care Unit, we would see our shadows on those walls.

And yet here we are these many years later, still loving him, wondering what his life would have been like. Our grief has softened. Gregory Peck, who lost a son, said in an interview once, "I don't think of him every day; I think of him every hour of every day." Lucas remains a living presence in our lives. When we travel, his picture comes with us. With the help of many friends, we set up a housing alternative for families with children being treated for cancer at Johns Hopkins. Lucas's name is on the door, and people who have found refuge there write us letters that we treasure. Like most bereaved parents, we have developed an abiding hatred for the word "closure." Many well-meaning attempts at consolation ("He's in a better place") demonstrate how little people understand. I have not been back to church since his funeral. Although I know many who have drawn comfort from their faith after such a loss, for me it would be a betrayal of my love for my son to imagine his dying as part of some divine plan.

His death has made my own easier to contemplate. I hope for a reunion with him even as I reject the faith that promises it. For a long time, I searched for him in crowds of children. Small boys with blond heads seen from a distance made me stop for a second look. I don't do that anymore. We could not move from our house, at least partly because we still imagined him finding us there.

I have fallen back on a belief in a kind of law of conservation of energy: People die but love is never lost. During his short life, he evoked in me feelings of which I did not know I was capable. That, it turned out, was his permanent gift to me. The process of mourning did teach me some things, however. It stripped me of the illusion of control, and I know now in a way that most people don't the futility of imagining that we have it. In a world where nobody gets out of here alive, we can take this truth as a reason for despair or as a way to mobilize the courage to get up each morning. Here is where we have a choice.

As my son's soul left his body, I imagined it like the balloons he so loved floating gently downwind. I thought I could not bear living without him or the thought of his being without us, and yet I have. As I now approach the western horizon of my life, it is with the fragile but persistent hope that my endless love for my little boy will dignify my existence and entitle me once more to hold him in my arms.

25

Ignorance can be remedied;
stupidity has no cure.

He who fights with monsters might take care lest he thereby
become a monster. And if you gaze for long into an abyss,
the abyss gazes also into you.

—Nietzsche

In February 2003, as we prepared to go to war in Iraq,
the space shuttle *Columbia* disintegrated, killing all
aboard. I wrote the following op-ed piece for our local
newspaper:

In our national grief over the loss of the space shuttle we
are in danger of overlooking some lessons from the

tragedy. It is inevitable that we glorify the dead astronauts beyond what they were: smart, courageous people, conscious of the risks but willing to take them to enjoy the thrill of being space travelers. That they were patriotic and dedicated to their jobs is beside the point. The applicants for such work are legion, and in preflight interviews the astronauts repeatedly characterized their experience as "fun" and "exciting."

An activity that requires people to travel 18,000 miles an hour with re-entry temperatures in excess of 3,000 degrees is obviously dangerous and unforgiving of any malfunction. There is enough history of mechanical mishaps in the 42 years of the space program to have killed 10 astronauts before *Columbia* disintegrated.

The investigation into the cause of the disaster has just begun. No doubt the experts will find something to explain it; they always do. But does anyone think that we have seen the last fatality in our exploration of space? As we push on to Mars, the risks increase and, thankfully, there will always be people eager to take them. The eventual pinpointing of the cause of the disaster will, as with the *Challenger* explosion in 1986, reassure us that some correction will be made to make future flights safer.

But, as Ernest K. Gann observed about aircraft crash investigations, "Sometimes we are left only with the feeling that some malevolent genie unzipped his pants and urinated on the pillar of science." As with all human creations, there are limits to technology, and there exists considerable potential for error in our most sophisticated machines. System redundancy, prior reliability, and the best quality-control mankind can devise do not ensure perfection. This is worth contemplating as we prepare for a war that we expect will be a triumph of American technology. But the video-game quality and 100-hour victory in our last military adventure in the Middle East may not be repeated.

We go into space because we are a curious people, committed to exploring the frontiers of our universe. This need is among the most compelling human qualities. It is a sign of our optimism that we assume that we can overcome all obstacles that stand in the way of our goals. (There is evidence to the contrary from the war of my generation, but it is unfashionable to mention Vietnam these days.) And we are willing to take casualties to get what we want. We see them as the inevitable, if regrettable, cost of being the world's superpower.

The war on which we appear about to embark carries with it a huge risk of disaster: Arab backlash, widespread death and destruction, environmental catastrophe.

Following the Sept. 11th attacks, our grief was laced

with bewilderment. How could this have happened to us? Much the same response was on display this week when the space shuttle came apart. There is an arrogance implied in such a reaction. Unexpected death from terrorism and from technological failures has been a fact of life for a long time and promises to be part of our future.

We may need a change in attitude in which we spend less time and emotional energy on puzzlement at our vulnerability to random calamity and more on acceptance that we live in a dangerous world. We may need a determination to learn what we can from what happens with the knowledge that perfect safety will always elude us.

What we should respect most about the *Columbia* astronauts is that they died in the pursuit of peaceful and humanly useful goals. They represented not just the best among us; they embodied our better selves.

Those of our sons and daughters who may be about to die pursuing a process of unimaginable destruction are equally brave, well-motivated, and infinitely precious. Do we really want to ask this of them?

26

Heroism is sometimes stubbornness in the face of adversity.

The Alexandria City Council voted unanimously yesterday to erect a privately financed $250,000 memorial to Vietnam prisoner of war Humbert Roque "Rocky" Versace, despite opposition to locating it in front of a busy recreation center.

—*Washington Post*, January 14, 2001

When I received an e-mail in 2000 announcing a Veterans Day ceremony in Alexandria to honor Rocky Versace, I knew I had to go. (That's "ver-SAIS"; he wasn't a fashion designer.) Rocky was in my company at West Point. He lived just down the hall for a couple years. I liked him. He was a big, muscular guy with a sweet disposition, which meant a lot when I met him because I was a lowly Plebe and he was an upperclassman with a license to make my life miserable. I always appreciated the fact that he didn't. In fact, Rocky was a little uneasy about himself. (I think this modesty accounts, at least in part, for his ultimate heroism.) In an environment that put a premium on aggressive, self-confident behavior, Rocky was unpretentious. Neither supremely intelligent nor gifted with what West Point saw as outstanding leadership qualities, he sticks in my memory as straightforward and determined with a strong Catholic faith and a knack for saying odd things. In 1958, our company was chosen to go to Washington to participate in the interment in Arlington National Cemetery of the Unknown Soldier from the Korean War. The parade would cross Memorial Bridge. When we were being briefed on the route, Rocky raised his hand to ask, "Should we break step crossing the bridge?" (He was referring to the practice of troops not marching in step across small wooden bridges to avoid damaging them with the vibration.) Naturally, the question was greeted with hoots and guffaws and was seen as typically Rocky, earnest and a little out of it. That's how I remember him.

Rocky's life after West Point was brief. In 1962 he was

assigned as a Special Forces adviser to a South Vietnamese unit in the Mekong Delta. They were ambushed; he was shot and captured. He was imprisoned by the Viet Cong in the Ho Bo woods, a huge swamp. He immediately tried to escape, dragging himself along because of his wounds. They recaptured and tortured him, but he attempted escape again and again. The VC, like good Communists, attempted to indoctrinate him in their philosophy. The incentives for cooperation were obvious, but Rocky would have none of it and just argued and argued with them, eventually in their own language. We know this because my classmate, Nick Rowe, was captured about this time and held in the same area. Nick escaped after five years imprisonment and wrote a book. He said Rocky was obstinate and suffered mightily for it. After two years, the VC executed him. I remember first hearing this story after Nick's escape and thinking, "Yep. That's Rocky. Stubborn."

Some of his friends from long ago felt that, in a culture that accords heroic stature to people who play games, Rocky's sacrifice deserved more recognition than it had received. They lobbied the military to award him the Congressional Medal of Honor, and they asked the city of Alexandria, where he had lived as a boy, to memorialize him in some other way. The first attempt was to get the school board to name an elementary school after him. He lost out for this honor to the late civil rights attorney Samuel Wilbert Tucker. Finally, the City Council was persuaded to give space for a privately funded memorial at the Mount Vernon Recreation Center. A design competition was held and a sculptor selected. Then a Veterans Day ceremony was scheduled at the Center to honor Rocky and preview the memorial plan.

When I showed up, the place was being picketed by a half-dozen people from the surrounding neighborhood. The scene was a prescription for discomfort: a bunch of aging white soldiers coming to establish a memorial to one of their own in front of a recreation center in a black neighborhood. Nobody wanted to make a racial thing out of it. The picketers (and later speakers in front of the City Council) talked about the "lack of community involvement in the review process." The white guys invoked patriotism and the dubious hope that the children using the center would find ennobling the statue of Rocky with a couple Vietnamese kids.

Pete Dawkins, the most famous undergraduate of my generation, gave the keynote. He was sixty-three, but he still looked fit enough to win that Heisman Trophy all over again. I played a little hockey with Pete a long time ago, but he didn't remember me (he was good; I wasn't).

Heroism is sometimes stubbornness in the face of adversity.

When he left the Army as a Brigadier General, he went on to become a "master of the universe" on Wall Street. He made a run for the Senate from New Jersey and lost. Now, here he was, speaking about his classmate Rocky. He called him "hugely courageous and indomitably spirited," which Rocky certainly was, though I doubted that he and Pete had been "good friends"; I just couldn't see them moving in the same circles at West Point. But you have to make allowances at a memorial service.

Other highlights of the ceremony included a couple choral numbers by some kids who use the center and an agile dance on the political tightrope by the photogenic mayor of Alexandria, who declared that he had "objected to that war" though not, he hastened to add, to "the participants." (I can almost see the road sign: Vietnam Participants Memorial Highway.)

Into this curious patriotic mix came Miss America 2000, who led us in "God Bless America," the anthem that Rocky is reported to have loudly sung when he was isolated as "incorrigible" by his captors. Improbable by war-story standards, but it *does* sound like something Rocky might do—both to keep up his spirits and to annoy the VC.

The ceremony concluded with a passable rendition of "Taps"—always a risky undertaking for a bugler in front of an audience that has heard that mournful call played well and poorly on so many evenings in so many distant places. We adjourned to the vestibule to see a model of the memorial, and then departed into the cool fall sunshine, passing the demonstrators who looked at us across a gulf of race and time and memory. They wondered, no doubt, as we did, "What are those people thinking?"

EPILOGUE: After years of efforts by his friends and classmates, the Army finally awarded Rocky the Congressional Medal of Honor.

27

Life is not a spectator sport.

The world is a dangerous place.
Not because of the people who are evil,
but because of the people who don't do anything about it.
—Albert Einstein

Most acts of power-based violence occur in the presence of others. This is especially true in social settings such as bars or parties on college campuses in which men frequently behave in predatory ways toward women. A large number of sexual assaults involve the consumption of enough alcohol to impair a woman's ability to consent. In situations like these, the sequence from the point of view of the man involves "target identification," superficially charming and flattering behavior, drinking to lower inhibitions and increase the woman's vulnerability, and then moving to a private setting where the sexual contact takes place. Because the initial phases of this sequence occur in public, usually other people can see what is happening. How they react is the key to whether a sexual assault occurs.

The largest group of bystanders consists of those who remain passive and rationalize what is happening as "none of my business." We observe the same phenomenon elsewhere when a majority of people who witness violence or some other form of injustice do not intervene. A common example would be an adult hitting or rebuking a child in public. Most of us have been present when this is happening. How many of us have done anything to stop it? The question is how much risk are we prepared to take on behalf of a stranger? People's explanations for not getting involved often revolve around fear for their own safety. But this fear does not explain many people's reluctance to make even a risk-free phone call when a violent crime is being committed in front of them.

Perhaps the most famous incident illustrating bystander passivity in the face of violence was the 1964 murder of Kitty Genovese in New York City. A young woman was attacked on the street at 3 A.M. for over half an hour while an undetermined number of witnesses failed to call police in the face of her screams for help. In 2010, Simone Black, a woman from the United Kingdom, posted a suicide note on her Facebook page. None of her 1,082 Facebook friends responded effectively and she went on to kill herself.

The "bystander phenomenon" is well known experimentally in the field of social psychology. The number of spectators present at any incident seems to be important: The more witnesses to an event that invites intervention, the less likely people are to act. A kind of diffusion of responsibility apparently occurs that causes each person to assume that someone else will intervene. We all also depend on social cues to decide whether to do anything. If one is in a group witnessing an act of violence and no one else is interceding, we are less likely to take action individually.

Whatever the explanation, our failure to help people in distress is a form of cowardice that ought to be addressed, especially in settings such as college campuses, where sexual assaults of women that begin in social situations is a pressing problem. Training programs are now being designed to alert people to the phenomenon that tends to freeze us when we are faced with circumstances in which another person is in danger. Although we cannot expect everyone to throw themselves in the path of an oncoming train to save a stranger, most situations requiring bystander intervention are physically less risky and more slowly developing, so we have time to consider whether to do something to stop what is happening.

A lot of attention has been given of late to the phenomenon of bullying, notably in school, though it can occur anywhere at any age. The intimidation of a weaker person by a stronger one usually takes place in the presence of others, and steps to prevent it invariably involve attempts to encourage people to intervene. Again, such efforts must overcome familiar dynamics in the bystander phenomenon: fear for one's own safety, diffusion of responsibility, a perception that certain people bring this misfortune on themselves, and the traditional need for scapegoats that many groups manifest. Teaching children that they have a responsibility to prevent the humiliation and coercion of another is difficult. It is even harder to convince adults not accustomed to taking risks to do so. The form of bullying called stalking is similarly receiving legal attention because of its sometimes lethal outcomes.

Life is not a spectator sport.

Most of the teaching that we provide our children on how to behave in the presence of strangers is cautionary and designed to keep them safe ("Don't talk to strangers"). Very little attention is given to how to confront situations in which a stranger needs help. These attitudes are the genesis for the reluctance of bystanders to get involved. Forces in the society that devote themselves to concerns about others are opposed by a culture of selfishness that argues that we must not risk what we have. There exist philosophical and political disagreements about the issue of our obligations to each other. So, for example, the homeless become invisible or annoying. When our capacity for empathy is breached, we become less attuned to the idea that any stranger in distress might be us or someone we love, so we turn away and go on with our lives. Our souls shrivel a little each time this happens.

28

One of the greatest risks is to be honest with ourselves.

If I am not for myself, who will be for me?
If I am only for myself, what am I?
And, if not now, when?

—Hillel

To claim any virtue, especially courage, we must manifest it in our behavior, the way we live. In an effort to seem closer to our ideal selves, we all employ some level of deceit in constructing the narrative of our lives. This habit becomes uniquely self-destructive when we begin to *believe* things about ourselves that are false. If we aspire to be brave, we must practice bravery in small ways so that we will be prepared when more is required of us.

The cardinal virtues are kindness and courage. Most of the other traits we manifest or seek to develop are derivative. From kindness, for example, come empathy, tolerance, and beauty. From courage, we derive honesty, loyalty, and optimism. In creating that version of ourselves that we present to the world, most of us would like to be seen as brave. It is common to invent an autobiography that contains examples of admirable behavior: athletic achievements, war stories, moments when we did something risky. On some Internet sites, you can purchase medals for valor to wear as if earned.

We search so hard for heroes to inspire us that the word *hero* itself has lost much of it meaning. But still we recognize, at least in the abstract, that taking risks on behalf of others deserves recognition.

As we inventory our own lives, we are sometimes surprised at how safe and comfortable they have been. The riskiest thing that most of us are required to do is drive our cars. When we encounter circumstances such as a health crisis, we are often astounded, as if such misfortune was not a routine consequence of being human. Because risk brings with it excitement, some of us seek it out in the form of hazardous recreation or gambling. What makes these pursuits different from displays of courage is that no one else stands to benefit from what we do. We are simply increasing our own rush of adrenaline, like injecting a drug that produces a temporary euphoria.

So to the elements of choice and risk, perhaps we ought to add usefulness to someone besides ourselves as a component of true courage. In fact, this latter quality may be more important than the degree of risk to allow us to include in our heroic pantheon people such as inner-city teachers or skilled medical professionals. If, as I believe, self-absorption is the personal characteristic that most threatens our ability to live peacefully with each other, why not award valor medals to those who manifest their feelings of generosity, empathy, and obligation to others, even if they are not risking their lives in the process?

One of the ironies of the capitalist system is that the largest material rewards go to the most selfish and acquisitive among us while those who dedicate their lives to the benefit of others are customarily the least compensated. Of late, the political term used by those who would defend the interests of the rich is to refer to their wealthy constituents as "job creators." Could our language be further degraded or used to obfuscate the truth? (This trend appears to have started when the War Department was renamed the Department of Defense.)

Being honest with ourselves requires more than an unsparing inventory of our personal strengths and weaknesses. We must also try to speak to each other plainly about things that matter, so we have some bad habits to break. For example, any sentence from a politician that begins with the words, "The American people" (think, feel, want, don't want, will not tolerate, and so on) will be followed by the speaker's own thoughts, desires, or ideology. The use of euphemisms and the passive voice ("mistakes were made") is another tip-off that we are being lied to. If we elect to high office people who speak to us this way, we get the government that we deserve.

Although we all are prone to reworking our pasts to fit with our present needs, we cannot rewrite history: e.g., the Founding Fathers did not anticipate corporate financing of elections, gays in the military, or the right of every citizen to own an assault rifle.

One of the most necessary forms of courage to all of us, individually and as a society, is the courage to change. Time forces this upon us as we age, and we have few models of graceful acceptance. Our relationships with each other are regulated by a system of laws that also requires continual evaluation and evolution. In this process, certain permanent truths must guide us:

1. It is wrong to treat another person as an object.
2. We are all in this together.
3. The measure of any society is how it treats its most vulnerable citizens.
4. Fear brings out the worst in us. We must not yield to it.
5. If we lived forever, there would be no such thing as courage.

29

At the heart of anger is sadness.

Now is the time to understand more,
so that we may fear less.
—Marie Curie

As we try to make sense of and to derive meaning from our lives, we are impeded by the many losses, mistakes, and resentments that attend the human condition. To weave a coherent narrative from our experience, we are tempted to blame others for what has happened to us. On a personal level, this sometimes causes us to become "injustice collectors," in which complaint becomes our standard mode of communication. In escaping this perpetual aura of grievance, we have to both take responsibility for what happens to us and acknowledge the role of chance in shaping all our lives. Our ability to live in harmony with each other requires relinquishing blame and replacing it with the idea of shared fate and the spirit of compromise that acknowledges that none of us has a monopoly on the truth.

In my professional life, people come to me to change. Usually they are experiencing unwanted feelings such as anxiety and depression that have become so burdensome that they are interfering with their lives, especially their ability to relate to others in a satisfying way. The mechanisms they have adopted to cope with these feelings—denial, avoidance, blaming others, self-medication—have not worked. In fact, these efforts have commonly made things worse. Because they do not know where these feelings have come from, they have no idea how to get rid of them. They would like some advice and imagine that I can give them a medicine or set of directions that will make them feel better. They are frequently impatient. They have been watching therapists on television who seem to get to the heart of the matter in minutes. They have worked with other professionals with different ideas about how people change and have not been helped. I feel some pressure to perform.

And so begins what might be described as an educa-

At the heart of anger is sadness.

tional effort in the service of understanding, which, if all goes well, will lead to different behaviors and feelings—in that order. I try to convince them that an examination of the past that is as honest as our fallible memories allow will yield information that will help them in the future. And I attempt to hold them in place long enough so that we can develop a relationship, a sense of mutual confidence, even affection, that will give them hope. None of us put much stock in advice from strangers (though the popularity of self-help books suggests otherwise). Only when we know and respect someone do they have the "leverage" to make interpretations, ask uncomfortable questions, and encourage us to look below the surface of our lives. This sense of being understood is why the therapeutic relationship is infinitely more important than the therapist's theoretical beliefs about what causes people to change. A secret about psychotherapy (at least with me): To help someone, I have to like them, and they have to like me.

Complaint is not a useful or attractive way of relating to the world, which is why much of our political discourse is so unappealing. Instead of constructive ideas about what each of us can do to solve problems, most politicians and people who comment about politics prefer to blame the people they disagree with for what is wrong. Often this blaming takes the form of a sense of victimization, in which the other side is portrayed as seeking to oppress, deceive, or otherwise disadvantage the forces of reason and righteousness. These complaints can reach absurd levels, as when the white, privileged majority feels attacked by those arguing in favor of the wealthy paying more taxes or keeping government out of our bedrooms or making health care affordable for all. These feelings of being threatened by a changing society are among our most destructive fears.

The absurdity of these anxieties is demonstrated by the recent finding that the wealth gap between whites and minorities has grown to its widest levels in a half a century. According to census data, whites on average now have twenty times the net worth of blacks and eighteen times that of Hispanics ($113,000 vs. $5,000 to $6,000). And yet a significant segment of white society feels threatened and protective of their advantages. Our political discourse has been degraded by the rise of an angry and self-righteous segment of the population that thinks it is legitimate to impose their vision of the future by threatening to damage our political and economic systems if they don't get their way. This threat is but a short step from violence, which, for example, among some religious extremists has replaced peaceful protest in the area of reproductive rights. When hateful accusations replace reasoned discourse, then compromise, the basis for any democratic system, becomes impossible and all we are left with are statements of faith and assertions that some people are better than others in interpreting God's will. In this direction lies theocracy and loss of the freedom to follow the light of our own conscience.

The role that fear plays in this process is obvious. If we imagine that others wish to impose their will on us in the name of some belief system, we feel justified in opposing this process by whatever means necessary. If we feel the need to arm ourselves to constrain the power of our own government, we have lost some basic trust that our voices will be heard and that we can effect change by peaceful political means. If we believe that our president holds office illegitimately because he was not born in this country, we are making a statement that is not just divorced from provable reality but is also a fear-driven, delusional rejection of our system of government. Like all conspiracy theories, it satisfies some fundamental need to see ourselves as victims who must resort to extreme measures to protect what we are and what we have against nefarious forces that would obliterate us. Such beliefs also imply contempt for those who disagree with us. Who can be tolerant of or seek compromise with people whom we are convinced threaten our very existence?

How can reasonable people argue against such fears? When treating patients in the grip of anxiety, a diffuse form of fear, logical argument has its limits. As I have commented elsewhere: *It is difficult to remove by logic an idea not placed there by logic in the first place.* In our political discourse, we see numerous examples of people behaving illogically, as when elderly people who benefit from Medicare and Social Security rage against government entitlement programs, especially universal health care, or people who buy guns after a mass shooting. Most of our fears are misplaced (remember the relentless advance of the killer bees?), but we are at risk of fulfilling them by our irrational reactions. The stock market, driven by fear and greed, oscillates wildly in times of stress and economic uncertainty. We engage in wars when threatened by stateless terrorists who respond to our invasions by moving their operations to other countries.

Just as in psychotherapy, in our political discourse there is no substitute for looking below the surface of the stories we are told, identifying the sadness and fear that underlies anger, the insecurity that expresses itself in ar-

At the heart of anger is sadness.

rogance, and the sense of meaninglessness behind most unhappiness. If we can apply this understanding to our political disagreements, we might be able to differ with each other with a little more humility and a little less certainty that only those who believe as we do deserve to be saved. And in this process, we might just find more to like and admire in each other—and in ourselves.

The quest for courage is a journey within.

The journey between what you once were and who you are now becoming is where the dance of life really takes place.
—Barbara DeAngelis

We assembled in March 1995 at San Francisco airport, a group of graying, overweight, middle-aged men. We were veterans of the 11th Armored Cavalry Regiment, Blackhorse, and had served in Vietnam some time between 1966 and 1971. We were retracing our journey into a war that none of us fully understood, then or now. We had survived to return to "the world," and made of our lives what we could. But unexpectedly, we carried Vietnam home with us and left some part of ourselves there. Now we were going back, each with his own story, each for his own reasons.

Accompanying me was my twenty-five-year-old Amerasian son, Michael, whom I had met as a newborn in Saigon near the end of my tour in 1969. I hoped that he might discover there something important about his connection to the earth and to that place. We planned some attempts to find his birthmother, but the success of this task seemed unlikely in the ten days of our trip.

On the final leg of the flight from Manila to Vietnam, I remembered having the same view, twenty-six years before, from the right side of a TWA 707. I wondered as we crossed the coast whether I would see, as I did in 1968, the moonscape of B-52 bomb craters that brought together in my mind our two great national adventures of the 1960s: the race to the moon and the Vietnam war, each so different in intent and result, one the signal success of my generation, the other our greatest failure.

As we made our approach to Tan Son Nhut airport, only peaceful villages and rice paddies could be seen. Was it possible that all signs of our presence there had been expunged like the filled-in bomb craters?

We stepped off the aircraft into blast-furnace heat, like

a living presence, that made us remember where we were. Before we boarded the bus to the hotel, we were approached by young Vietnamese women wearing traditional *ao dais* who handed us bouquets of flowers. Only later did I read that half the current population of Vietnam was not even born when last we were here.

The following day, we met some of our one-time adversaries at the Ho Chi Minh City Veterans Association. There were no hints of animosity and I thought this must be easier for them; they had won, after all. Gifts were exchanged and we each received a small oil lamp used by the VC to light their bunkers and tunnels, most of which we never found. That lamp sits on my desk as I write this.

The next day, I took Michael to the Tu Du Maternity Hospital, where he was born. With its stucco walls and treed courtyard, it looked exactly as it did when I found him there so long ago. Although we failed in our attempts to locate his birthmother, I think that just coming back to the place of his birth was enough for this visit. He made a connection and vowed to return.

We boarded a tour bus and began our journey into the past. We went first to Long Binh, a huge American base during the war. Nothing is left; it has been obliterated. I remembered the hospitals, a giant Post Exchange, swimming pools, even a Chinese restaurant—all gone. We stopped at the site of our old Blackhorse Basecamp. The place is peaceful now, with widely spaced houses adjacent to a Vietnamese military complex. Some of the veterans, dropping to their knees, were able to excavate artifacts from our time there: an unexpended .30-caliber bullet, a rusted C-ration can, a couple short lengths of barbed wire. One of the group put a little of the coarse soil into a film canister to take home.

I broke away from the main body and spent a day alone in a van traveling to the area of operations where the most intense combat I recall took place. I found some of the villages I remembered. I wanted to see if the bullet-pocked monument in one of them memorializing the local soldiers who died with the French in their own lost war in Vietnam still stood. It was gone, part of the cleansing of the country of all traces of both us and our South Vietnamese allies. I remember that monument as providing an epiphany for me. How could we succeed where the French had failed thirteen years before? How much like them we must have looked to the people of that village.

The guide turned to me at one point and asked hesitantly, "What do you think of the MIA problem?" This was not the last time I was asked that question by English-speaking Vietnamese. I finally understood their mystification that the 1,617 American soldiers and airmen still missing were such a barrier to "normalizing" relations between our two countries. The American preoccupation with our lost countrymen, especially the fantasy that some may still be POWs, seems odd to the Vietnamese in view of the fact that more than 300,000 North Vietnamese and Viet Cong troops remain unaccounted for. "I think they're dead," I responded. The guide nodded sadly and told of the family members of MIAs she had accompanied to remote villages, where they vainly asked after their loved ones.

We stopped next in Ben Suc, the hamlet leveled in Operation Cedar Falls in 1967 and site of the memorable explanation by an Army officer to a TV reporter: "We had to destroy the village in order to save it." We traversed the infamous Iron Triangle, pausing at the remains of an American M-48 tank of the sort we used in the 11th Armored Cavalry. It was curious to see the veterans climbing on it. An "I rode with the Blackhorse" bumper sticker was irreverently affixed to the main gun, like an effort to console ourselves at this tangible symbol of our defeat.

Roads and airfields are the only permanent signs of our having been there. Pierced steel planking with which airstrips were covered is now in evidence in backyard fences. Old .50-caliber ammunition boxes serve as flowerpots.

The quest for courage is a journey within.

In Tay Ninh, we stopped at the Martyr's Cemetery, the resting place for twelve thousand Liberation soldiers, their equivalent to our Arlington. We laid flowers and burned incense. The ceremony brought one of our guides, Col. Can, to tears as he remembered his son dead at Khe Sanh. His grief evoked something from all of us and each vet touched his shoulder or shook his hand as we reboarded the bus.

To visit the Cu Chi tunnels, only thirty miles from Saigon, is to learn why we lost the war. The elaborate, painstaking construction and concealment by the Viet Cong which extended over twenty years shows a determination that no amount of technology could overcome. The huge B-52 bomb craters preserved there are monuments to the futility of trying to destroy more than two hundred miles of tunnel that hid entire battalions of fighters while our tanks and infantry maneuvered above. In war, as in life, there is little that will not yield to persistence and a belief in time as a stream carving its way slowly through the rock of resistance. They did not need to win; they had only to endure until our Western impatience and moral uncertainty caused us to depart.

It was a relief at last to see the ground fall away and the coastline of Vietnam fade behind us. Some scattered applause from the veterans was reminiscent of the cheers on the departing "freedom bird" in 1969. This, I knew, was my last trip to the place that had such an effect on my life, on all our lives. I was filled with a sadness that I could not define. I was flying back to those who care about me, both for who I once was and who I am now. And whatever I left unfinished was Michael's to seek and find. I have, after all, had my time. Perhaps this was my regret. When I went there in my youth, it was to an adventure. I sensed that the war would be the defining event of my generation. My country was divided and I faced challenges both to my manhood and my humanity. Since then, I have grown old.

I think this return trip helped most of us, seeing Vietnam at peace and the people friendly and unafraid. Perhaps that is as much "closure" as we're entitled to. We can't bring back the dead, ours or theirs. We seem to be forgiven by those who remember us at all. We might as well forgive ourselves and come home at last, each with whatever separate peace he can attain.

The years have leached from us the passions of youth—misdirected as they were into war. On our journey, we failed at recapturing what we were and felt. The shape of the land has changed, as has the topography of our spirits. We vainly tried to orient ourselves with old maps, which no longer fit the ground on which we walked. The young people who took us from place to place must have wondered what we were looking for, not knowing what it is we remember. We carried the burdens of time and fate and our hearts were weighted with the knowledge of those who cannot return and whose stories are lost to all except those who loved them.

Acknowledgments

This book contains ideas borrowed from many people, most of them not known to me. Those I do know who have contributed to what little I have learned about the world—teachers, friends, patients—are too numerous to mention and many would not welcome their names in print. I am grateful to the people who have had a direct hand in creating this book: my esteemed agent, Rafe Sagalyn, my peerless and supportive editor, John Radziewicz, and his colleagues at DaCapo. The difficult task of copyediting was skillfully accomplished by Susan Pink. Christine Marra played her accustomed and important role in getting these words organized and into print. My daughter, Emily, took time from her efforts to save the world to bring her skilled editorial eye to the task of improving the writing. Tom Stacy, PhD, and Dave Gold, PhD, provided encouragement, friendship, and a day job when I most needed one. Tom Ferguson was the first to believe I had something worth saying. All errors of fact and interpretation are mine. I am hopeful that, as in the past, what I have written will be read with a forgiving heart. And thank you, Matthew Lore, for starting me down this road and continuing to be my friend.